Praise for @YourService

"Frank understands that one of the cheapest, most effective forms of marketing is called extraordinary Customer Service."
—**Seth Godin,** Author of *We Are All Weird*

"Compelling, personal, and illuminating, @YourService is a delight to read, and essential if you have any influence at all on how your own company manages the Customer experience!"
—**Don Peppers and Martha Rogers, PhD,**
Coauthors of *Extreme Trust: Honesty as a Competitive Advantage*

"@YourService talks about what Customer Service really means in the networked world and helps you get there. It helps you face the changes you need to make in your corporate culture to realize the benefits of superior Customer Service. There's lots on the technology required, but the focus is always about how people treat people."
—**Craig Newmark,** Customer Service Rep and
Founder of craigslist

"Eliason shows you how to enchant your Customers by building trust and likability with the small, personal touches. His wisdom is bound to make your business flourish in this new age of fast, free, and ubiquitous social media."
—**Guy Kawasaki,** Author of *Enchantment* and
Former Chief Evangelist of Apple

"At Zappos, we believe that if we get the culture right, then most of the other stuff, like delivering great Customer Service or building a long-term enduring brand, will happen naturally on its own. This book shows the clear impact that company culture can have on the Customer experience."
—**Tony Hsieh,** *New York Times* Bestselling
Author of *Delivering Happiness* and CEO of Zappos.com, Inc.

"Too often Customer Service is seen just as a cost. But what is the cost of a lost Customer or a ruined reputation after the ex-Customer talks about it online? In @YourService, Frank Eliason shares hard-won insights from the front lines of the online Customer Service revolution he helped pioneer. Through real-world examples and folksy anecdotes Frank illustrates the simple truth that bringing decision makers closer to Customers and empowering lower-level employees to deliver improves consumer experience, and the bottom line. Simply put, it pays to be nice, because when every Customer can be a publisher online, the potential costs of doing anything but are too dear."

—**Ben Popken,** Former Managing Editor of Consumerist.com

"As someone who had spent a career moving through sales, corporate strategy, marketing, and corporate communications, I thought I knew something about Customer Service, or at least the importance of Customer Service. I had always railed against my marketing colleagues for seeking Customer acquisition, but forgetting about Customer retention. Frank Eliason not only understands Customer Service, but he has also made it into a real profession in the age of social media. Frank helped teach the people at Comcast how to reach out, engage, talk with, listen to, win over, and win back customers. His ideas have spread to other companies. He is, in my opinion, a seminal figure in the field of Customer Service. As someone who cares deeply about connecting strategy and execution to build and grow brand and reputation, I celebrate Frank's accomplishment as the one who helped teach companies about how Customer Service is integral to brand and reputation. This is a book well worth reading!"

—**Elliot S. Schreiber,** Clinical Professor of Marketing
and Executive Director, Center for Corporate Reputation,
LeBow College of Business, Drexel University, Philadelphia

"Frank has learned the hard lessons and speaks from the heart when it comes to Customer Service. In @YourService he gives vital information to all who need to cut to the chase and learn the return on investment from outstanding Customer connections."

—**Marsha Collier,** Author of *The Ultimate Online Customer Service
Guide: How to Connect with Your Customers to Sell More!*

"Every business wants to know how using social media can improve its bottom line. One of the simplest answers is told here beautifully by Frank Eliason: In the age of the networked Customer, a real-time, human approach to service can save you money, improve your brand, and build Customer equity that you can take to the bank. Don't miss this book!"

—**David Rogers,** Author of *The Network Is Your Customer:
5 Strategies to Thrive in a Digital Age*

@YOUR SERVICE

@YOUR SERVICE

HOW TO ATTRACT **NEW CUSTOMERS**, INCREASE **SALES**, AND **GROW** YOUR BUSINESS USING SIMPLE CUSTOMER SERVICE TECHNIQUES

FRANK ELIASON

WILEY

John Wiley & Sons, Inc.

Published by John Wiley & Sons, Inc., Hoboken, New Jersey.
Published simultaneously in Canada.

For general information on our other products and services or for technical support, please contact our Customer Care Department within the United States at (800) 762-2974, outside the United States at (317) 572-3993, or fax (317) 572-4002.

Wiley publishes in a variety of print and electronic formats and by print-on-demand. Some material included with standard print versions of this book may not be included in e-books or in print-on-demand. If this book refers to media such as a CD or DVD that is not included in the version you purchased, you may download this material at http://booksupport.wiley.com. For more information about Wiley products, visit www.wiley.com.

Library of Congress Cataloging-in-Publication Data:

Eliason, Frank, 1972-
    At your service : how to attract new customers, increase sales, and grow your business using simple customer service techniques / Frank Eliason.
        p.   cm.
    Includes index.
    ISBN 978-1-118-21722-1 (cloth); 978-1-118-28688-3 (ebk); 978-1-118-28393-6 (ebk); 978-1-118-28231-1 (ebk)
        1. Customer services.   2. Corporate culture.   3. Customer relations.   I. Title.
HF5415.5.E57 2012
658.8'12—dc23
                                                                                    2012003419

Printed in the United States of America

10   9   8   7   6   5   4   3   2   1

I would like to dedicate this to my wife, Carolyn, and our girls Gia, Lily, and Robyn. Thank you for supporting my dream to see the Customer Service field come to a seat at the table for every business. I could never have taken my first steps on this path without you.

Contents

Foreword

I thought Frank Eliason had a terrible job: handling complaints from Customers for the largest company in a much-disliked industry, Comcast.

But he did wonders. He fixed Customers' problems. He doused a bonfire set by a well-known grump (I'll let Frank tell you about ComcastMustDie.com). But most amazing—with humor, directness, and credibility—he put a friendly, human face on a cold corporation.

He did it on Twitter. While many other companies were just discovering social media and using it mostly as a promotional platform for their institutional messages, Frank used his Twitter name, @comcastcares (picked, I'd like to think, with just a dash of irony), to talk with Customers, to listen first, and to build relationships. He lived and worked the precepts taught by that seminal work of Internet culture, the "Cluetrain Manifesto," now a decade old, which decreed that markets are conversations; conversations are held among people, not institutions; and we Customers can hear the difference.

Frank brought his company back from the brink of its own Dell Hell. I should know. I'm the Customer who unwittingly set loose a consumer firestorm on Dell when I complained on my blog—these were the ancient days before Twitter—about a lemony laptop. Dell at first ignored the complaints of bloggers, but after a year, when Michael Dell returned to the company's helm, it dispatched technologists to fix grousing bloggers' complaints. It blogged with a human voice. It set up a service, Ideastorm, to capture and implement Customers' ideas. In social Customer Service, Dell leapt from worst to first, setting a model for many to follow, including Comcast.

Frank has since moved on, from cable to banking (or some might say, from the frying pan to the fire). And Customer Service as a trade is also moving on with new tools introduced regularly to help companies track and respond to complaints, sentiment, and memes about them traveling through the net at broadband speeds.

But this isn't a craft—and Frank's isn't a story—of technology. It's a story of people. It's about returning to the days when people at companies knew Customers by name and Customers could name people in companies. It's about a resurgence of accountability. It's about the kinds of sensible, courteous, and decent suggestions Frank gives you here to build honest and productive relationships with Customers.

Productive. That, I believe, is the next phase in this rapidly evolving field of social Customer Service: moving past complaints to collaboration, moving from putting out fires to building new products together. In my book, *Public Parts*, I tell the story of Local Motors, a company that collaboratively designs and builds cars. Now that might sound absurd, but it works so well that the company is not only producing cars—together with Customers, making design and business decisions—but the company is also in a position to help even big car companies learn how to make Customers partners.

When Customers are treated with respect and given the right tools to connect with companies—with the people inside companies—then amazing things can happen. That's really the moral of Frank's story about his relationship with Customers.

One more note: By day, I am a journalism professor at the City University of New York. As such, I will confess that I cringed when I saw Frank capitalizing the word "Customer" at every reference. The copyeditor in me wanted to correct them, to make each lower case. But Frank will explain why he does this, and he won me over because we are all Customers.

—**Jeff Jarvis,** Author of *Public Parts*

Foreword

At Your Service versus @YourService

Dear Customer,

I saw your Tweet about how upset you were with your experience with our product. I didn't see it live, but someone forwarded it to me via e-mail on my BlackBerry. I guess what was delivered didn't meet your expectations. Hey, it happens to everyone. But, you sure did let us know in your own way, didn't you? Come to think of it, you let everyone know. So what was originally something between you and us is now everybody's business.

I don't get it though. Sure your time is valuable. It's so valuable in fact that you chose to avoid the various systems we invested significant time and money in to address these types of issues. Hey, our time is valuable too. That's why we spent millions on technology to automate our systems and responses. We didn't divert profits toward this expensive voice recognition software because we didn't want to be close to you or talk to you live, but to make it a more efficient process. That says something about how much we value you, right?

It doesn't stop there though.

If you make your way through the series of prompts and redirects, we've hired and trained a staff of people who are prepared to address you directly. And guess what . . . if they can't fix your problem, they have backup resources in locations all around the world to step in and attempt to resolve the issue. Sure each individual will ask you to start from the beginning and retell your story, that is, if you do make it to one of them, and assuming you don't get disconnected. They do, after all, want to make sure to hear every detail of your experience from the very beginning. Also, please excuse their brashness. Everyone works hard, we all have somewhere to go, and you're probably not the only one having a hard day.

So, next time you think about Tweeting, blogging, Facebooking, Googleing, YouTubeing, Pinteresting, Yelping, Foursquaring, or whatever social whatchamacallit-dot-com you decide to vent on, remember, if you want resolution, the best path between two points is a straight line. Call us. E-mail us. Fill out a trouble ticket on our website. We're here to help. This is an "A" and "B" conversation so you're so-called social network friends can "C" their way to funny cat videos instead.

If you want us to come to you, to respond where your attention is focused, where you are connected to hundreds or even thousands of people, you should connect with our "community manager" because we're busy helping those Customers who follow our rules. But you see, they're just working here part time. She is the niece of one of our executives who's helping our company with the social media plan because she has free hours in between classes and she is on the Twitter. We have a few people who work with her in between their stints as entrepreneurs. Some have profiles in Facebook, one uses Myspace, and another person has his own channel on the YouTube where he reviews other people's YouTube videos.

To be honest, you're better off not working with them. Not only do our traditional channels have technology, we have years of established rules, processes, and even internal reward systems that make sure we get to you when we can, how we can, to ensure that your time with us is endured and rushed.

Between our rules, our systems, and our people, we want you to have the most efficient experience possible so that you are a happy Customer, a loyal Customer, and ultimately an advocate to convince other Customers to buy our products. You get a solution, we get someone in our PR department to work with you on a success story, and oh, our Net Promoter Score will go up too. It's a win-win! See now how that social media just gets in the way of a good relationship?

Now, how may I help you?

Allow me to answer on your behalf. No, better yet, please allow me to Tweet this on your behalf. Businesses must adapt the service infrastructure to meet the needs of you and me—the connected Customer. Not because they wanted to; because they have to. As individuals, we are gaining in influence with every connection we make. And when we share experiences, we contribute to a greater collective of experiences for anyone with a search box to find. And take a guess when that search box really hits a business below the belt . . . that's right, when another potential Customer is searching for the posted experiences of others. That's why we're influential. Individually and collectively we influence the decisions of others simply by sharing our experiences.

Why do we take to social networks to voice our problems? Businesses might be surprised. It's not just about resolution, it's about whether or not businesses are living up to their promises and whether or not they're investing in the Customer relationships stated in the almighty mission statement hidden somewhere on their website.

We're empowered, and we don't take this authority lightly. When given the opportunity to wield our influence for fairness and a sense of service, we will take to every network where we can prompt resolution or transformation.

It's more than that, however.

This is nothing short of a consumer revolution. We've had it. Our hope for recognition and value from the myriad of businesses we've supported over the years had turned hope into despair. Our faith in the system was eroding until we took measures into our own hands.

This isn't about upsetting the balance. This is about introducing equality in the relationship between Customer and company. So, not only is the Customer always right, but the Customer is always right—right now. This is the real-time web and we are venting to get your attention, to earn support from our community, and to change systems that are outdated. And, if you want a win-win situation, by paying attention to us in our networks of relevance, by connecting with us in the moment, you will end up creating a new model supported by technology, people, processes, and metrics that facilitate efficient and effective direct engagement. You build a better way while connecting with the very Customers that define your success. And, you invest in relationships in the process.

The result? Well, it doesn't take a rocket scientist to figure this one out. It actually takes a social scientist. This is about relationships. And to invest in relationships requires a commitment to improving experiences and increasing empathy. This is a time for innovation in how you engage with Customers now and over time and how you measure and appreciate the aftereffect. This is *that* moment to create a culture of Customer-centricity and employee empowerment to enliven a more engaged, informed, and vested front line of stakeholders . . . to rekindle your company's promise and deliver a meaningful experience before and after every transaction.

If you acknowledge that someone is in need, that mere action communicates how you value Customers. There's tremendous value in extending your hand, albeit digitally, and it only invites appreciation and reciprocity. By providing resolution and seeing the engagement through to satisfaction, you've not only invested in a relationship, but converted a potentially negative experience into a positive outcome where one-to-one engagement will now reverberate across social networks through one-to-one-to-many connections. More important, by investing in positive experiences you influence the decisions and actions of others. Remember, shared sentiment is discoverable by prospects and as they discover these experiences, those shaped by your engagement, the resulting decisions, of course, net in your favor.

These are emotional landscapes and this is why expressing that you care is so vital. The negative sentiments of dissatisfied Customers will not cower into the digital corners of the social web simply because you plug your ears, close your eyes, and shut your doors to engagement simply because it doesn't align with your current service directive. When you do engage, however, well the world of experiences is yours to define. And thus, the future of business is not created, with Customers, it is co-created.

Delivering exceptional Customer Service is the new way businesses will grow. But that means more than asking, "Would you refer us to someone else?" It means asking or observing whether not Customers actually *did* refer your business to someone else. More important, that they did so across their social networks.

This is why, as Frank Eliason so eloquently explains, businesses and organizations everywhere, must be @YourService if they are to continue to earn the business, support, and influence of their Customers.

In your corner and in the corner of your Customers,

—**Brian Solis,** Author of *The End of Business as Usual* and Principal Analyst, The Altimeter Group

Acknowledgments

Where do you begin when there are so many people you would like to thank? Throughout my life I have had many ups and downs, but each experience and personal interaction has added value. Our history makes us who we are. Let me start by thanking everyone who has influenced me over the years, especially family, friends, and coworkers.

I am grateful for every Customer I have ever had the opportunity to interact with. You may have thought businesses were not listening, but I can assure you that I was, and I always shared feedback. I have been lucky to work with many extraordinary people over the years, but I do not have the space to thank each one individually. I do want to acknowledge some key people who have been very special and really added value to this book. Specifically, I would like to acknowledge the late Carol Anderson, from my first job in high school. At Vanguard Investments and Advanta bank, I learned the importance of mission and the importance of the employee culture. The people at both institutions continue to inspire me. At Citi, I have worked with many people who instill this similar inspiration, including Tracey Weber, Michelle Peluso, Paul Michaud, Mike Cardace, Anna O'Brien, and Lara Ruth.

At Comcast, I had the opportunity to work with many who influenced me. I am particularly grateful to my digital care team members George Lunski, Bill Gerth, Melissa Mendoza, Vinisha

Chugani, Sherri Carson, Mark Casem, Steve Teow, Detreon Roberts, Bonnie Smalley, and Kim Pollard. They are an impressive group to work with. Additional Comcast team members I was privileged to work closely with Tina Waters, Nicole Patel, Rich Roberts, Rick Germano, Scott Westerman, Mike DeCandido, Dan Gallagher, Jenni Moyer, Scott McNulty, Jorge Alberni, Jen Khoury-Newcomb, D'arcy Rudnay, David Cohen, Steve Burke, and so many others. To Brian and Ralph Roberts, thank you for the opportunity and for building a great team.

My family has been through so much over the years, especially with many years of my working nonstop. To my wife, Carolyn, thank you for sticking with me through the roller coaster we have been on. I love you with all my heart and I promise to put down the phone and show that more often. To my Angel, Gia, thank you for inspiring me with everything you did. Through your life you have connected me with so many around the world and provided strength and courage that I remember every day. To Lily and Robyn, thank you for the energy and the fun escape you provide to me. I look forward to you growing up in a world where you know you can make a difference when you put your mind to it. I would be remiss if I did not thank Keurig for keeping my coffee cup filled, via Lily and Robyn, while writing this book. My parents, Frank and Joan Eliason, have served as inspirations, especially in business, throughout my entire life. I have always sought my own path, but one I hope you could always be proud of. My in-laws, Dale and Jane Meier, have inspired me: not only through their amazing children, but also in the way they live their lives.

I also want to provide a special thank you for my friends Lisa and Randy Hawkins. Ever since the day we met in the NICU, I have been inspired by both of you. Your advocacy for your family is nothing short of astonishing. Janet and Rich Napoli, words cannot describe the impact you have had on my life. To me, both of these families are a part of my family.

Last, but certainly not least, I want to thank all those who work in the Customer Service field and strive to create the right experiences for their Customers. I am always inspired by outstanding service. Please realize that having the right passion will help you move forward in your career. You have the power to make the difference, one Customer interaction at a time.

1

This Could Be Your Brand

There are some things in life that you just can't make up, so I will start by sharing a real-life social media case study that is playing out on the Internet as I write. The story is powerful and could easily happen to your brand. We are starting with a story that is intended to educate you on the impact your Customer can have. I am not looking to trash the individuals involved; in fact, in the way I see it, this could easily be your brand or mine. In any case, I am not a gamer, but I love what this product and brand stand for and I think you will, too. I am hopeful that Customers and potential Customers will look past this incident and bring success to the company involved.

Have you ever heard of Kotkin Enterprises or David Kotkin? Kotkin Enterprises was founded by Dave Kotkin and they make unique game controllers. According to CBS 4 in Miami, Florida,

David was an art teacher at Holmes Braddock Senior High School in Miami. A student wanted to use his new game system but had trouble due to a skin condition. David went to work and created the Avenger controller, an attachment over the existing controller that the student could use. It is an amazing story of success in America. There was a need and David was able to invent the solution.

David had been an inventor for years and had sold some of his inventions to others. However, with the invention of the Avenger controller, he decided to build a company himself. Like many other small business owners, David did not know all the ins and outs of business, so he hired experts to help him, one of which was a marketing firm David hired to help him get the Avenger into stores as well as answer Customer inquiries.

Kotkin Enterprises first introduced a controller for the XBOX. Here is how the Avenger controller is described on their website:

> The Avenger is an external adapter that houses the existing XBOX 360 controller, helping to improve your situational awareness, accuracy, agility, and reaction time. The Avenger allows for rapid, fluid movements between individual buttons and analogue sticks. Equipped with a stabilizer stand, customizable levers, high-precision tension straps, hair-trigger capabilities, and sensitivity adjusters, the Avenger can be fine-tuned like an instrument.

After the success of that product, Kotkin Enterprises began launching a new controller for Playstation 3. Due to delays in manufacturing, Customer preorders did not go out in the originally promised time frame. A Customer named Dave (not to be confused with "David" Kotkin), excited about the product, decided to e-mail the company regarding the status of his order. The marketing firm hired by Mr. Kotkin handled the e-mail interactions with the Customer. What happened during this interaction has been a learning experience for Mr. Kotkin and one that I hope will help you as well.

Dave is an ordinary Customer, like you or me, who simply paid for a product that he wanted to receive in time for the Christmas holiday. The original purchase had a promised delivery of early December, which had come and gone. Dave waited until mid-December, more than a month after placing the original order, to contact the company about the status of his order, which was for two controllers. His original e-mail included feedback regarding the fact that he was forced to pay upfront for a product that had not shipped. Kotkin's marketing firm replied to Dave, saying that the product was still in China. Then, Dave responded to clarify that he most likely would not have the product in time for the holiday. The next exchange from the marketer to Dave stated that the controllers were now in the United States.

Suddenly the conversation took a wrong turn. The Customer replied, questioning a new discount that was being offered to new Customers. Dave inquired about canceling his original order and placing a new order to get the discount. The marketing firm representing Kotkin responded with, "No one is allowed to cancel and reorder; if we catch anyone doing that, we will just cancel your order altogether."

As you can imagine, this exacerbated the Customer and he replied with a rant about the overall experience and the treatment that he had received as a Customer. The Customer also researched the marketer and shared feedback regarding some videos that he was in, not related to the product, as well as outlining all of the issues he had had until that point. This Customer response then generated one of the oddest responses I have seen from any businessperson: The marketing firm responded with an outline of a number of connections the firm has in the press and gaming community, and makes many personal attacks on the Customer, including stating that Dave is "the douchiest of them all [in relation to all the others with similar complaints]." Please note that I do not use or approve of this sort of language, but have included it here to stress the magnitude of the situation. I think that this is unacceptable in any form, but from a business perspective, I am floored.

Throughout this exchange, several individuals had been copied on the e-mail chain. The latest e-mail grabbed the attention of one of the recipients, Mike "Gabe" Krahulik, the artist for the popular website Penny Arcade. Gabe is also the founder and organizer of the popular Pax Events, an event at which Kotkin Enterprises had hoped to have a booth. At this point, he entered the conversation, making it clear to the Customer and the marketer that this company would not have a booth at the Pax Event. This led to more e-mails from the marketer claiming how great the product was doing and listing all of the upcoming events that they would be part of. The marketer also went on to claim a number of connections that he had in the industry, going so far as to state that he would be able to get a booth regardless, because money and connections can go a long way. Gabe reiterated who he is, inferring that the marketer might want to Google him and reference his popular website.

Gabe posted the story on the Penny Arcade website, and it spread like wildfire. The e-mails themselves are very damaging to the Avenger brand and Kotkin Enterprises, but this is certainly not where the story ends. In fact, it is just the beginning.

In the new world of @YourService, everyone who is in contact with your Customer impacts your brand. It does not matter if they work directly for you, a public relations (PR) firm, a marketing firm, or an outsourced Customer Service center. The Customer does not care, either; to them, it is still your brand.

In just twenty-four hours, the story spread to more than four hundred websites, and thousands of tweets. Over the next few days, it grew exponentially, even making it to many traditional news outlets. At first, the marketer saw this along the lines of "any press is good press." The marketer then reacted the way many other businesses tend to do when their brand has been damaged: threaten legal action. (Probably not the best attempt to make this sort of event go away!)

The marketer eventually e-mailed Gabe at Penny Arcade asking him to stop spreading the story. Gabe responded with an important lesson. "The reality is that once I had posted the e-mails, I didn't have the power anymore. The Internet had it now and nothing I said or did was going to change that." The marketer did offer a half-hearted apology to Gabe, as well as a press conversation with a similar tone, stating that he had not realized how popular Gabe was and that he didn't believe he was really Mike Krahulik. Let's face facts: This situation was not caused by the actions of Penny Arcade or its popularity. This was solely due to the marketer's responses, which were in writing, to a Customer.

At this point this story took on a life of its own! When a story like this becomes popular, people everywhere will start to dig into all facets of the company or situation. One of the first things discovered is that much of the content used on the marketing firm's website is completely plagiarized, all the way to their About Us page. The firm blames this on outsourced foreign creators of the website. Then, some of the people whom the marketer had referenced as knowing in his e-mails to the Customer and to Gabe started to come out and state that they, in fact, did not know him. Many also offered their own opinion of what had transpired. Once trust has been lost, it is very hard to gain it back.

Later in the book, we further explore the Kotkin Enterprises case, including their response, which was highly effective. The company did quickly tell the website Kotaku, "We apologize for our poor representation from [Marketing Firm]. We wanted to give [individual marketer's name deleted] a chance. He was rough around the edges, but he had drive and enthusiasm. However his behavior was unprovoked, unnecessary, and unforgivable. We are no longer represented by [Marketing Firm]."

At face value, I feel badly for Dave Kotkin and the entire Kotkin Enterprises team. They hired a firm that they believed could bring success. The marketer was obviously energetic and passionate; unfortunately it was probably not for the brand, product, or Customer, but instead for something else. As this unfolded, the ratings for a product not even released yet dropped on Amazon from four stars to one star. Marketing firms with similar names soon felt repercussions because their brand was unintentionally being trampled.

In the past, Dave may have shared his story with the press or other organizations, but the impact to the brand most likely would have been minimal. Most often, journalists or other organizations might simply forward the story to the company. It was rare for these stories to become part of the news cycle, let alone reach into the heart of your Customer base and energize them, as is now happening on the web. We are going to continue to discuss the Kotkin Enterprise story, along with many others. I hope you enjoy the ride and gain value for building your own business, no matter the size.

Welcome to Our World of @YourService

Thank you for taking the time to read *@YourService*. You will gain insight on how to succeed in this new hyperconnected, Customer-driven world we live in. I do not consider myself a writer and do not plan on taking the traditional approach to writing a book. To me, this, just like social media, is a conversation. We will continue the conversation online via Twitter using my handle @YourService. You will also find the conversation at FrankEliason.com.

Throughout the book, I share lessons that I have uncovered in the Customer Service business as well as recent examples, as I am now combining my service strength with the world of social media. Many marketers believe the world of social media to be a utopia that will sell their product and increase word of mouth. Because of this, people will sell you anything to improve your business using social media, but you most likely already have the right tools to win.

The first thing you have to realize is that there has been a shift in the way that products and services are marketed. The control resides in the hands of your Customer. Many will say that it always has, which sounds good but is not really the case. Previously, companies easily controlled, altered, and filtered their message as best they could through media and traditional marketing messages. Today, Consumers are talking to each other more than ever in loud voices. Winning them over will bring success to you and your business.

You do not have to believe me regarding this shift, but let me tell you how I shop for goods and services. I do not typically watch live TV and when I do I fast-forward through commercials, so that makes it difficult for marketers to reach me. Although I do surf the web often, I usually find the ads, especially page takeovers, to be annoying. So how do I buy? First, although I do still like to shop in old-fashioned brick and mortar stores, I usu- ally shop online. Regardless of whether I am walking through the store or shopping online, when I notice a product, my next step is always to visit Amazon and read reviews on the product. Sometimes I even take pictures of a product in a store so that I can research more fully at a later time. Next, I Google the product to see other reviews. I might also ask my friends for their recommendations. I then take all of this information and com- bine it with price info found from searching the web to make a decision. The shocking thing about this research is that it can all be done in a matter of minutes. The world is changing, and this understanding will help you win!

Some will say that I see the world with my own colored lenses on, but for me it has always been through the eyes of a Customer. I was lucky enough to have Bloomberg's *BusinessWeek* magazine describe me as "the most famous Customer Service manager in the U.S., possibly the world." But the way I really see myself is as a simple Customer Service guy. Over the years I have watched many employees fret about the dealings they would have directly with Customers. I have witnessed so-called leaders do what they can to avoid direct contact with Customers. How sad is that? If you are scared of your own Customer or shareholder, it is time for you to get into a new business.

So, before I begin, let me tell you a little more about myself. Like so many others, my career started in retail with firms like 84 Lumber, Macy's, and Lord & Taylor. Retail experience helped mold my many thoughts regarding service and the employee experience. More importantly, I saw the benefits of exceeding Customer expectations and delivering exceptional service.

One of the challenges to the retail world, especially in the mid-1990s, was that the work was nonstop, with managers putting in ninety-plus-hour workweeks. Needless to say, tensions could fly and I could not see it being a winning, long-term career strategy. This disappointed me because I had always loved the opportunity to serve Customers in person. After a few years, I decided to take a pay cut and a role in a call center selling guaranteed life insurance. I didn't last long in that role because of a takeover of the company and a restructuring of the department. Basically, the new company outsourced the entire sales department. To many a layoff is a horrible life event, but in this circumstance it was the best thing that could have happened. After this three-month stint and receiving a three-month severance package, I immediately found work at a company called Vanguard Investments. Vanguard, their founder Jack Bogle, the then-CEO Jack Brennan, and the noteworthy culture of the team would have a profound impact on my beliefs for years to come.

Around this time, other amazing things happened in my life. Most importantly, I married my beautiful wife, Carolyn. At Vanguard, I worked my way up through the ranks starting as a call center investment advisor and then becoming a retirement specialist. It was in that role that I began to be able to help thousands of people in an area that can be very difficult to understand with many legal and taxable decisions. To me, the most rewarding aspect of my job was helping other employees to create the best Customer experience, which I did through training and coaching individuals. Eventually, I had the opportunity to return to the management ranks that I had enjoyed during my retail days, as a supervisor in the high net worth area. This experience was extremely rewarding but also a time of great change that would impact my thoughts for years to come.

During this time, a life-changing event occurred in my personal life, which would be a great influence on my career decisions and become a guide to everything I do. My wife and I had our first daughter, Gianna Rose, or Gia for short. There are important aspects to what occurred that you should know as you read this book. Gia was not supposed to be born due to complications with the pregnancy. In fact, we were told to terminate the pregnancy, which we chose not to do. Gia was born prematurely at thirty weeks, weighing in at three pounds, fourteen ounces. She would spend the first months of her life in the Neonatal Intensive Care Unit (NICU) at the Children's Hospital of Philadelphia (CHOP). Needless to say this was a time of joy, yet a lot of stress. Family and friends, while well-meaning, constantly called for updates while we struggled to deal with the present. Back in 2000, there were not many family websites, but since I had helped others build websites, I built one for Gia as well. We could then send inquiring minds to the website to obtain updates, eliminating much of the stress we felt from our need to be in constant contact. This improved communications and made things easier for everyone. There is nothing that can prepare you to handle something like this, but we were surrounded by exceptional people who taught us to be passionate advocates for our child. Ultimately, I have applied this trait to my crusade as a Customer advocate.

In addition to being born prematurely, Gia also was diagnosed with cystic fibrosis, a genetic disorder that impacts lungs and the digestive system. Although labeled a life-shortening disease, many CF patients live long, healthy lives. Of course, people hear the diagnosis and immediately think the worst, especially if they do not fully understand the disease. Gia's website was a great way to educate others and share a positive message. Finally, Gia came home after two surgeries and three months in the NICU. Life was resuming some normalcy.

Throughout that time, Vanguard had been a great place for me, as I had a very supportive work environment and the privilege of working with some of the smartest, most Customer-centered minds around. But ultimately, I decided that it was time to move on. I chose Advanta, a small business bank near my home, because it would shorten my commute significantly and I could have more time with Gia and Carolyn. I had heard about Advanta from a colleague at Vanguard. He was so impressed by Advanta's culture that he hoped to return there.

As I had not had much experience outside of retail, I did not realize the dramatic differences in culture that occur from one company to another. This would all change during my first week at Advanta. At the time, the company had shrunk from being a powerhouse in financial services to being a small business credit card company. Up until this point, I was familiar with a culture that encouraged employees to question things, particularly if a process or procedure was having a negative impact on the Customer. At my new job, while I was listening to calls, I questioned an unacceptable action taken against a Customer. I took it to my boss to ask if this was normal and I will never forget the answer, as it was something I had never heard up to that point but have heard many times since. The answer was, "It is what it is!" This manager's answer was not because he didn't think that the action was unacceptable; in fact, he actually agreed that it was unacceptable. He had answered this way because it had been questioned in the past and the company's policy would not change. The bottom line was to shut up and go back and do your job. I was not in Kansas anymore!

During the next few years, I learned to drive change and really see the shortcomings in the service industry. I had the opportunity to work with senior leaders, guide direction, and strive to reshape how the company thought about service, even while outsourcing and in a climate of financial pressures. It was a lot of fun to be a part of, and I have always admired and cherished Advanta's employee-centered culture. At the same time, changing things for the better has always energized me and I was craving to do something bigger. Living in Philadelphia, the choice was easy: Comcast.

While all of this was going on, Gia was doing well. She was growing and it was obvious that she was as smart as could be. However, we continued to be uncomfortable and dissatisfied with her healthcare at CHOP. Shortly before Gia's third birthday, we decided to review other healthcare options in the area largely because we were very much interested in obtaining a device called "the vest," which is used by CF patients to shake mucus out of the lungs. Although used in adults for years, it was just starting to become popular with children as young as three years of age. The CHOP team did not support it, despite the promising research available, and the main challenge was obtaining insurance approval for a device with such a high cost. We found our way to A.I. duPont Hospital for Children in Delaware. There, the pulmonary team supported the vest, and they were committed to helping their Customers obtain insurance approval. One of the first things the team did was review the plethora of medications that Gia was taking. Among them was one for CF liver disease, which is not typical for children as young as Gia. They asked some questions about how long she had been taking it, which had been from the time she came home from the hospital. Then, they asked if an ultrasound of the liver had been done to determine if she in fact had CF liver disease. We were not aware they could even test that. Of course, we asked for this procedure to be done, and the results were unexpected. Tests could not confirm CF liver disease, but they did find a tumor on her liver. This tumor ultimately proved to be a cancerous tumor known as hepatoblastoma. We were in for an all-new round of dealings with hospitals.

Again, we turned to Gia's website to help educate people about the cancer and we kept them up to date regarding Gia's care. By this time, the web was becoming a popular means of sharing stories with family members, and in some cases, complete strangers who were interested. Websites were popping up all over to help families dealing with diseases, such as cancer, speak to their family and friends. One notable example is Caringbridge, which allowed us to connect with families like us on a global scale. We were already doing this in the CF community, but the childhood cancer community was a powerful asset. We were learning from each other, identifying treatment options, and sometimes finding a virtual shoulder of someone who really understood what we were going through.

The cancer treatments went on for almost a year, culminating in liver transplant surgery at Johns Hopkins Hospital in Maryland. I am heartbroken to report that Gia did not make it through her liver transplant surgery, passing away two months before her fourth birthday. My wife and I saw an outpouring of support from every continent on the globe. People told us how they had found our website and had kept up on Gia's care throughout the ordeal. It was an extraordinarily emotional time and one that still impacts us every single day. Gia helped connect us to many around the world, her story touched many, and the experiences are reflected in everything we do.

I will be forever grateful to the donor, their family, and all who are willing to donate their organs to give others new life. Organ donation is the most generous gift that we can give. Please consider becoming an organ donor!

In September 2007, I left Advanta and joined Comcast. My role was managing Comcast's executive complaint department. I was excited about the opportunity to work with senior leaders to help shape the Customer experience going forward. I had not had a love affair with Comcast prior to joining the company. In fact, in many ways I despised them, and it was not even their fault. My frustrations with the cable industry had started when I bought my home. The installation, which should be an easy process, took more than a week because the cable company did not have a piece to connect the line at the street. Of course, my opinion had also been clouded after my cable provider had shut off my cable two weeks before I even moved out of my previous apartment. Overall, I had not had good experiences with my cable provider, Suburban Cable. I was so frustrated that I bought and installed a satellite service instead, cancelling my service with Suburban Cable. Eventually, Suburban Cable was taken over by Comcast, but in my mind I transferred that blame to Comcast, even though as a company, they had had nothing to do with my previous experience. When high-speed Internet became available, I did have to return to a cable provider because my home was not eligible for DSL from my phone company. But as soon as DSL was available, I canceled my cable subscriptions and vowed never to return. After dealing with both satellite providers and eventually Verizon Fios, I realized that cable, if they were to change and become more Customer centered, could easily win. Of course it would require change! Anyway, I now was working for Comcast and determined to be successful.

Although I have been given credit within social media for changing Comcast, the fact is that the change required many people and the perfect storm to ultimately drive change. I am thrilled and honored to have had the opportunity to play a small role. When I started there, the company was in the midst of crisis. If I recall correctly, I started on September 5, 2007, and on September 9, Bob Garfield, an *Advertising Age* writer and National Public Radio host, posted a blog titled "Comcast Must Die." This multipart post on his *Advertising Age* blog was the beginning of a major rant that would be only one of a few crisis moments to strike. We had to figure out how we would respond as a company. Now I was part of a team that would set out to completely change the dialogue internally and externally. What Bob Garfield did not know was that we were looking up people who posted negative comments about our company on the blog, identifying them, and reaching out to try to assist them. When I joined Comcast, I thought my team would be servicing Customers, but really they were message takers who would send a ticket to the local market for assistance. In my view, this created a disparity for how Customers would be treated from one location to another. Each area was run very distinctly, causing a wide range of Customer experiences.

Bob Garfield's "Comcast Must Die" posts gained momentum, and he moved it to a standalone blog. This was not the first crisis for Comcast within social media. About a year prior, a person had posted a video of a technician falling asleep while on hold waiting for Comcast service. This video, seen by more than 1.5 million people, would lead to significant changes within the company. In addition, there was another incident that had occurred in late August when a seventy-five-year-old grandmother, Mona Shaw, had taken a hammer to one of the Comcast offices after growing extremely frustrated by her experience. I stumbled upon a real-life crash course in public relations, communications, and the impact service has on the brand. There is nothing like learning by fire. Many leaders from diverse areas within the company, including PR, marketing, and the regional businesses would start to lead the change. They saw the negative impact on the brand and the team really lit a fire to create change and get things done. We had to find short- and long-term solutions to improve the brand. We created a plan that worked and is continuing to change the organization. Will people ever love their cable company? Probably not, but the changes that we created will help the brand and create improved Customer experiences. It will take a long time for people to see all of the changes, and if you have not already, you will notice them over the coming years.

As you will see, history makes us who we are and has a great influence on how we think and what we do. This insight will not only help you throughout this book, but in the very human world in which we live where personal connections are key to success.

Today, my wife and I have two beautiful girls named Lily, age five, and Robyn, age four, and after Comcast I returned to the banking industry with Citi. Citi is another large organization and the industry is ripe for changes. My role is in marketing, but my heart will always be in Customer Service. As you read this book, you will notice that I see social media as an equalizer for the Customer, allowing them a greater role in how an organization is operated. So no matter where I sit, my role is to represent the Customer and advocate for the experiences they desire. This is how you win in this new hyperconnected world, and through the pages of this book you will discover how you can drive that change in companies big and small. We will have fun along the way, sharing more stories and building understanding that fits in today's business environment. Of course the views that I express are solely my own, unless stated otherwise, and they are not those of companies who have or currently employ me. In the coming pages you will learn to:

- Connect the dots internally.
- Present data in ways that have impact and drive change.

- Identify value no matter where your Customers are talking.
- Build human connections.
- Create an environment where Customers want to share your story.

Beyond this we also help to identify failures that exist today, ways to correct them, and ultimately build the service experience that most executives believe they already offer. Ultimately the future is all about being @YourService.

CHAPTER

3

It Starts with a Capital C

The English language has a lot of rules, especially regarding capitalizing a word. Here are some rules for capitalization:

- The first words of a sentence
- The pronoun *I*
- Proper nouns (the names of specific people, places, and things)
- Family relationships (when used before proper names)
- The names of deities (Exception: Do not capitalize the non-specific use of the word *god*.)
- Titles preceding names, but not titles that follow names
- Directions that are names (North, South, East, and West when used as sections of the country)
- The days of the week, the months of the year, and holidays

- The names of countries, nationalities, and specific languages
- The first word in a sentence that is a direct quote
- The major words in the titles of books, articles, and songs
- Members of national, political, racial, social, civic, and athletic groups
- Periods and events
- Trademarks
- Words and abbreviations of specific names

Isn't it interesting to see where our language places priority? Family relationships make sense, but how about members of national, political, racial, social, civic, and athletic groups? The Philadelphia Eagles are extremely important to me, so it can make sense. We use capital letters to emphasize something that is important. The name of a business is important, so why not the Customers whom they serve?

Every word you communicate is important, whether directed to your significant other, a colleague, boss, vendor, or your own Customer. Words, and the way that they are presented, tend to play an important role in setting the tone. I started to capitalize Customer when I worked for Vanguard Investments. The people who invest in their mutual funds own Vanguard. Here is how they describe themselves and the interests that they serve:

> Most investment firms are either publicly traded or privately owned. Vanguard is different: We're client-owned. Helping our investors achieve their goals is literally our sole reason for existence. With no other parties to answer to and therefore no conflicting loyalties, we make every decision—like keeping investing costs as low as possible—with only your needs in mind.

Vanguard has a culture centered on their Customer. It all stems from their founder, Jack Bogle, who many in the investment community believe is a leader like no other. Jack was highly opinionated regarding investing and is considered the founder of index investing. Jack was chairman of Wellington Management Company when he was fired. This was shortly after a merger in which the existing Wellington team had lost some control. After the firing, Jack did something very different. He approached the boards for the Wellington Funds (many people may not realize that the company has a board and so does each mutual fund) and proposed a new structure for service and support. This led to the creation of the Vanguard Group. Vanguard is owned by the funds, so every penny of profit went back to the fund, creating much lower expenses compared to other fund companies. Today, Vanguard's average expense ratio is close to 0.21 percent compared to the industry's around 1.15 percent. That is a big difference. So, as you can see, Vanguard was truly set up for the Customer. The culture and ownership of the company was centered on the Customer right from the start. The culture is most prevalent in something they call the Swiss Army, which I explain in a moment.

I did not realize until after I had left Vanguard how much fear Customers can create in the eyes of employees. I have always enjoyed interactions with Customers, especially in person. I now realize that many employees of other businesses do not feel the same way. Would people in your company take calls from Customers? Would your CEO? There is a culture problem at companies when people are scared of their own Customers. Part of this problem is the identity crisis that the Customer Service field has always had and the ability of those within it to set the right tone internally. The reality is that Customers are the reason any company is able to exist. The basic aspect of business is having products that people want and are willing to pay for, to obtain value or return for shareholders. Ultimately without the

Customer you would offer no value for your shareholders, so Customers are key! The problem is that the culture within service departments often leaves a bit to be desired and employees are striving to get out. This is because most of the company leaders unintentionally send messages that service is beneath them. We tend to talk down to service or not even care about their needs. Many companies completely outsource Customer Service, which sends a clear message to the Customer and employees alike. They seem to believe that it is not important to be close to your Customer. Well, this is not true at Vanguard! Vanguard's Swiss Army requires employees to take calls during busy times and a minimal amount throughout the year, even when not busy, to keep the skill up to date. All levels within the company, including the CEO, take calls.

Think about the business impact if all your employees were taking calls from Customers. What decisions would be made differently? Would you have the same policies or procedures that you currently have? Based on experience, I can assure you it would be very different. The Customer's story is an integral part to winning in this social world.

Vanguard uses their Swiss Army to instill this culture but it is also a way to flip the leadership funnel. Too often, companies are built on a top-down structure. This is not usually the intent of the CEO (with some very notable exceptions) but many think of leadership as command and control. This may work for some businesses or people, but not always. In fact, I think that it can have an opposite effect. Right within their call center, Vanguard has an area reserved for Swiss Army volunteers. The area is set up with phones, computers, reference material, and most importantly, call center employees who help the executives get through the toughest of calls. They are trained like all other Customer Service personnel, but since they do not use the skills as often, there are team members there to help. It is an honor to be asked to help out the Swiss Army. How often does a call center employee have the opportunity to help the CEO or any other senior executive taking calls? I have seen many careers take off, simply because of a casual chance encounter when someone is provided the opportunity to share their expertise. Can you imagine the CEO dealing with a difficult policy and someone right by their side explaining the impact that policy has had? Change happened each and every day at Vanguard because of these simple conversations taking place in the Swiss Army.

The Swiss Army was also a great place in the company for fodder and folklore to grow and thrive. There were numerous stories, most probably false, of calls handled by various executives. One such tale was about Jack Brennan, the CEO at the time, speaking with a Customer who wanted to escalate to a higher authority and refused to believe Jack was who he said he was. There were stories of the Index Fund managers discussing a no phone exchange policy that existed to prevent day traders from taking advantage of short-term fluctuations in the index that in turn would cause long-term investors to have added trading costs to meet the money movement. The stories may have been folklore, but they helped to instill a belief that the senior staff truly did understand the difficulty that phone representatives dealt with each day.

If you work in the Customer Service world, this will be a story that you can probably relate to. If you do not, this will help you understand the disconnect that happens between Customer Service and the leadership of an organization. I have seen surveys of CEOs and other senior leaders showing that they believe that they are providing the best possible service, when in fact their Customers are unhappy. Did you ever wonder how this disconnect happens? I know! While working for a senior Customer Service leader, I had the privilege of helping prepare topics for a meeting with the leadership team. Let me tell you about this preparation in detail.

First, we had to find the perfect call. Back then we did not have modern call recording equipment, so we basically used old-fashioned tape recorders. We would peruse hours and hours of recordings to find a call. Usually this took about twenty hours just to find three calls to take to the senior leader for consideration. Inevitably the senior leader would review the calls and each would be rejected for some small detail. "We can't share that topic," or "I did not like the tone here," or some other minutiae. So back to twenty more hours of searching for the perfect call. It was so hard at times that the senior manager would actually have us create the perfect call. Of course, the CEO truly believed that we had a world-class call center. Since I have worked at a world-class call center, I knew that we were far from it.

Over the years serving in call centers, I have heard all kinds of calls and had the opportunity to work with amazing service representatives. Each type of call that I have heard provided a learning experience for the organization and for me. The best calls might validate some information or show a better way to talk about something. The worst calls, although people often blame the representative, were often the worst because of the topic, our own talking points, or the process involved. Digging into these calls with the representative involved helped to pinpoint where the core of the trouble was.

Many companies have listening programs, but that is not nearly the same as actually taking calls and experiencing the human emotion that goes with them. These listening sessions are often highly choreographed events. The calls chosen may be on set topics, but the content is balanced even if that is not reality. So if a manager shares a bad call on a topic, it would be balanced with a good call. All this is part of human nature. No leader wants to share a bad experience created by their team. They feel like they are the ones personally responsible. The challenge to that way of thinking is that it has also caused us to avoid some very necessary conversations.

Even listening to calls with a representative can skew perception. When leaders come to listen to calls, many service teams will seat the observer with the best agent available. They may even make sure that the other agents sitting in the area are at the same level.

Certainly I am not expecting every company to feel enlightened and set out to copy Vanguard's culture, but I hope that you will realize that in the socially connected world, whether your organization is transparent or not, others will identify your culture for you. This culture will define your brand for years to come. It is ultimately your culture that will be part of the equation to winning or losing. One of the key ways Customers identify the culture is based on their interactions with your brand. What do you think your brand represents to them?

4

Do You Tell Your Customers Not to Call You?

Obviously no business is going to fess up to telling Customers not to call, but it happens! Wouldn't it be refreshing to hear a company just come out and say, "Your call is not important to us"? I know that this is not realistic, but, on some level, I would applaud the honesty of it. Often I call places and this is the message that I get even if it is not the words that they are using. Companies send a lot of messages unintentionally. You would expect service to be a fundamental aspect to how we do business, but it really is not. For many companies, the Holy Grail is figuring out how to get Customers to pay for items without servicing the Customers' needs. It is probably not a good long-term strategy but unfortunately many aspects of business are built on short-term expectations. The average tenure of a CEO is less than seven years, so, depending on the nature of their business, the CEO might not have it in their interest to have you repeat purchases.

Remember that we are all human, which opens the door to many amazing feats but also many common pitfalls, including caring what people think about us at any given moment. But, ultimately, Customer Service does not fall strictly on the CEO because, truthfully, they are probably not even fully aware of the problem.

When companies were smaller, CEOs were close to the Customer or the employee on the front lines. But today we are in a world of large, multidimensional global businesses. There may be multiple types of Customers and the company itself may not have a direct line of sight to the end Customer.

I have always been fascinated by the space race in the 1960s. In a world of turmoil, there were many focused on John F. Kennedy's mission to place a man on the moon before the decade was out. The spirit of innovation was everywhere within the world of NASA. I am amazed at all the technological break-throughs that came out of NASA at this time. Today we take many of them for granted. We all know the folklore story of President Kennedy visiting Cape Canaveral and asking a janitor what he was doing and the janitor responding, "I am sending a man to the moon, Mr. President."

Where has the sense of mission gone within the Customer Service industry? For the most part it has been completely missing. Years ago service was simple; it was composed of one-on-one interactions. Over the years we added technology to the mix with phones or mail. From the 1960s to the 1990s, we saw a big boom in call centers, and new technology was quick to follow. First came the 800 numbers, and then call routing, and then everyone's favorite invention, the IVR, or the automated voice response (press 1 to be ignored, 2 for voice mail, 3 for the incorrect department, etc.). We were forced to create new procedures to handle faxed correspondence. Technology allowed us to start doing many more things, but, of course, the more ways we do things, the further distanced the Customer feels. The technology has continued to grow more sophisticated and easier to use, yet the Customer does not feel important. How do you feel? Not within your company but when you are in the Customer's shoes maybe getting service for a product that you bought? Do you get frustrated by long wait times? My favorite (and I say this facetiously!) is the IVR that does not let you get through to a human being. Since I have worked in the industry, I tend to call after exhausting all other options and only when I absolutely must speak to someone. Businesses tend to make it extremely difficult to get a live person on the other end of the phone. Fortunately, we are starting to see the trend move away from some of that. Some companies are touting not having an IVR as a reason to buy their product.

Now let's talk about self-checkouts. Do you opt to use them? I personally prefer using them, but they are not for everyone, nor should they be. To me the decision to have them available should depend on the Customer's preference. This has been a problem for some companies who have opted to rely solely on self-checkout, forcing people to do something they do not necessarily want to do. That is the issue that needs to be addressed, not the technology itself.

Recently I purchased a new home, moving closer to New York. When you buy a home, you tend to do a lot of repairs to get it just right. This, of course, meant countless trips to home improvement stores. I think that my local Lowe's and Home Depot must know me by name as I have been in so frequently this year! Anyway, I was in one of the big box retailers and I witnessed self-service at an all time low. On this day, due to the size of the items that I was purchasing, I avoided self-checkout and went to a cashier. As the cashier rang up my items, she found that one of the items in my cart did not have a UPC sticker. Although I was shocked when the cashier asked me to go to the complete other end of the store to get another item with a UPC, I ran back to the aisle to pick it up. I figured that it was probably faster than calling another employee over and waiting for him to find the item. Regardless, I was understandably miffed at the cashier's unawareness that making this request created a very poor Customer experience.

You should never have to ask the Customer to do something due to any process flaw. Like many other people, I chose not to provide feedback. I have had many good experiences at this particular store so I am sure it is not representative of what they teach their team members. However, a few days later I was in the same store and I saw another example of rock bottom service. All of the regular checkouts were closed and the only checkout open was a self-checkout. For my purchase I personally did not care and would have gone that direction anyway, but in front of me was an elderly gentleman who was not experienced using self-checkout. I watched for close to ten minutes as he struggled trying to complete his purchase. I was tempted to go over to assist him, but the employee would go over every few moments, help with one thing, and then step back. The employee was simply doing the bare minimum to show the Customer how to use the machine. In this circumstance, the employee could and should have completed the sale for the Customer or at least along with the Customer. It is highly unlikely that having mandatory self-checkout was a corporate decision; most likely it was a decision made in that store based on the number of cashiers available and how slow it was that evening. Regardless, self-service went way too far. This is a constant problem today at many companies, even at some that are known for the service they provide.

One of the key reasons for this disconnect is that the service world has been trying to gain an identity. Unfortunately within most companies, service departments have been seen simply as a cost center. To counteract this, many service centers committed to become sales centers. The thought was that we are talking directly to our Customer, so we can easily drive sales. So, now when you call companies, you are bombarded with extras. "I know that you are calling because this item is broken, but can I sell you an extended warranty while I am talking to you?" This conversation gets old real quick. It also sends the message that we are not here to help you; we just want to sell products to you. This problem has extended to even some of the best brands.

For example, I had a frustrating experience a few years ago when I called a company that I knew from experience has a world-class Customer experience. I was calling due to a fraudulent transaction that I had just noticed. Although nice and pleasant, the representative had to transfer my call in order to have the transaction reversed. Before she would or could transfer me, she had to offer services or extras. She offered their mobile app, which if she had had accurate, current information she would have known that I already had this product because I had seen the fraudulent transaction using this service. The rep went on to offer other services that I already had and used. I was extremely frustrated, annoyed, and agitated, so I asked to be transferred.

My time is valuable and I expect companies, particularly companies that I do business with, to recognize and respect that. It is not difficult, but many companies have made these calls into a process, and her procedure said that she had to offer certain items prior to closing out the call. Most Customers prefer you to take care of their reason for calling first, and then if appropriate, ask about special offers and new products later. Years ago, Verizon did this really well when I had their landline service. When I would call, which was not often, they would address my reason for calling and then ask if they could review my account. At the end of these calls I felt like I had bought more service, but I was always pleased. I felt they were valuing my time and focusing on me, instead of their needs. It may only be a subtle difference, but to the Customer this focus brings much more dedication to the brand and the service experience. In your interactions with Customers, where is your focus?

Another challenge in call centers is how things are measured. Many call centers still measure agents on handle time. For those of you not familiar with call center jargon, this is typically the amount of time spent talking to the Customer, time the Customer is on hold, and any after-call time to complete the tasks. This is one of the performance metrics that are very common. Would you mind if I stood behind you all day with a stop watch and timed everything that you did? Then told you to be faster? Now imagine if you were the Customer and the person whom you called for help was rushing you? That is exactly why this is a bad metric, and call centers are filled with poor forms of measurement.

I remember one call center director who was proud that he was not measuring handle time but instead focusing on calls per hour. I am sorry, but there is no difference. Then, as call centers started to outsource, we started something even worse than measuring handle time. We started to enforce the use of scripts.

Scripts sound great in theory, but how do you feel when someone is reading a response to you? Do you trust that they have an understanding of your situation? Did they listen to what you said? The other challenge to scripts is that the Customer does not have the other side of that script so they are at a disadvantage, as they could not possibly know precisely what to ask. Scripts often come from people who have never spoken to a Customer and do not understand what they represent to the Customer. Remember that all Customers are unique and in some ways so are their situations.

While at Advanta, we decided to rethink the Customer interaction model. We did this across the board so it included web, phones, e-mail, chat, collections, outsourcing partners, and Customers. Out of all I have accomplished, I am still most proud of the work with this team. We threw out all prior ways of running a call center and we built it from scratch. One of the first things we did was to change the metrics. Gone was handle time, replaced with a Customer survey based on the call experience. We did not survey the Customer immediately after their call because that tended to skew the results. We did it after forty-eight hours so that they could make sure the call was handled as the Customer had expected and they did not have a need to call back due to our own failure. We found some amazing statistics. Customers rated longer calls lower than shorter, more efficient calls. When we had first introduced this concept to agents, we told them to just focus on helping the Customer to avoid the need for the Customer to call back. They did just that. Handle time did go up by twenty seconds, but repeat calls dropped significantly and Customer satisfaction increased dramatically. As we rolled it out to other teams, the same phenomenon happened. The increase in handle time lasted for sixty days, then returned to normal, but other metrics, such as Customer satisfaction, stayed at the new level.

At the time we were making these changes, I was the manager for Quality Assurance and Customer Satisfaction. This meant that my team was the typical call center team that usually enforced employees following the process, such as selling new products and services to the Customer and that agents closely followed scripts. That was never the right approach to quality, but when you look at everything from a process perspective you might have thought otherwise. We changed procedures to measure behaviors found in a call. We also got rid of all scoring, so agents were not graded for the call. As we made these changes, we evaluated the needs of our employees. They wanted to be trained to be successful. We also evaluated what our managers were doing, and most often they were doing anything but managing or coaching. In our view, the most important part of their job was just that. So we redistributed work and had them focus on what was important: their people. We then coached the managers to focus on developing only two or three behaviors that were identified during the monitoring process as opportunity areas. The managers would focus on these trends until new trends developed. We were quickly creating a strong service team focused on the Customer.

We duplicated the changes that we made internally with our external partners, which is the nice way to say offshore, out-sourced call centers. There, the changes took time to take effect due to the focus of their management team and the metrics that were within their contracts. Once that had all been worked out, the changes had the same impact.

We focused on feedback from all of our agents regarding policies and procedures and we constantly talked about improve-ments generated by their feedback. Every time they identified improvements we would see more excitement, enthusiasm, and energy throughout the call center. Now, the voice of the Customer is not new, but many companies collecting this feedback fail to follow up on it. While I was at Vanguard, I learned how moti-vating this follow-up was, especially to agents. At Vanguard we had a database that collected this feedback and everyone received responses based on the feedback. We created and implemented the same process at Advanta. We also included the agents in meet-ings where we reviewed the feedback, and we made sure that they were included in project teams established by and resulting from feedback. They were part of every step of the process.

We also flipped the funnel on quality! As mentioned we stopped scoring agents, but we did start grading the company as a whole. We began to study various topics, which would allow us to grade decisions made in other parts of the business in terms of how they affected Customer Service. During this effort, we implemented new, advanced call recording technology from Verint systems that converted the speech in the calls to searchable text. Now we could search and find calls on any topic, build dashboards on it, and share the story in a deep way. The quality team was the advocate for the Customer within the organization and they were able to drive change throughout the company as a whole.

In today's Customer Service world we are constantly sending messages to our employees and Customers. These messages are now having a severe impact on our brand, but by rethinking the basics, or often getting back to the basics we can create the message we always intended. Building a new call center culture is not hard but being @YourService will be a key way to win!

5

Let Me Check with My Boss

Although your telephone call may not be the most important thing to most companies or their representatives, they would certainly like you to carry their positive message about the brand to the social media world for them! Give me a break. The reality is that companies struggle to understand social media because they think of it as any other marketing initiative such as TV or print. They think that they can force you to see their message, but this is far from reality. We are still in the early stages of social media, but some of the early wins by companies may be sending the wrong message. If you want to succeed with social media, you first have to create the right experience through your other Customer touch points. You have to have the right products, great service experiences, and something that people will want to talk about before you can be successful through social media channels. The most hyped about brands in social media create their experiences through other channels or more importantly, through their employees and/or Customers.

One of the most discussed brands on the Internet is a favorite of mine, Apple. As a company, Apple is talked about much more than any of their competitors, by dramatic margins. I know many companies have been talking about Apple in recent years, especially with the death of Steve Jobs, but they are most discussed for a reason. Their products are usually strong and fit into one's life. They are easy to use and do not have many issues, viruses, or troubles. For this we pay a premium, and if you are like me, you pay for it over and over again as they launch new products or enhance existing ones. They have also been known to create a mystique around their products, especially during Steve Jobs' tenure. I hope that they will be able to continue that.

However, they also have another strength that is not talked about as often, but that leads to strong Customer advocacy, which is the reason I mention them here. Beyond their beautiful and highly functional products, they have created an amazing buying experience through their Apple stores and more importantly, impressive service experiences through the Apple Genius Bar. Through this easy and comfortable experience, they are able to get you more entrenched in their products, becoming part of their world. Because of this, I credit my dedication to Apple products to an Apple store employee at the Genius Bar in Ardmore, Pennsylvania. He helped me on two occasions, both times creating an experience that I am still wowed about years later. During the first experience, I had just bought an iPad and somehow it got dented during my travel; it looked like something had chewed it. I took it in to get it repaired. The Apple employee looked it over and then went into the back room. When he returned he explained that he was sorry, but they would not be able to fix it. He also thanked me for being a valued Customer.

Next, he surprised me by handing me a brand new iPad and saying, "Have a nice day!"

During another visit, I took in an older Macbook because the DVD drive had broken. It was out of warranty and I knew that I would have to pay to fix it. I waited my turn and in the process I helped another Apple Customer who was having difficulty with their computer and the Internet. Through the conversation I was able to identify a fix so that their Comcast service would work with their Apple computer. The Apple employee was amazed that I had taken the time to help another Customer. Of course the interaction caused the wait for my time slot to be much longer, but it was personally satisfying to be able to help another Customer. The Apple employee thanked me profusely for helping the Customer. After this, I told him about my work at Comcast and how he could get hold of my team if he or his Customers needed assistance. Finally, I showed him the trouble with the DVD drive. He returned and said, "Thank you for helping our Customer and as a sign of appreciation we are going to fix the DVD for free." He apologized when he explained that this would take a week. The very next day I received a call that it was fixed and ready to go with a new DVD drive. At that time, I owned three iMacs, a Macbook, the iPad, and an iPhone for work. Today, I have two more iPads, three Apple TVs, two Macbook Airs, and one Mac Mini Server. I credit and thank this employee for my dedication to this company. As an Apple fan, I enjoy talking about their brand and have posted on Twitter, Facebook, and Google+. In addition, I have written blog posts about them. Apple never ceases to amaze me with products and outstanding service. Apple has created a loyal and dedicated Customer not only in me, but in millions of people around the world!

The key to the Apple success story is their highly empowered team. Most service personnel have limited abilities to get things done. They have a process that they must follow and are not permitted to deviate from. Successful service teams take an alternative approach empowering individual employees to do what is right.

Ritz-Carlton is another great example of employee empowerment. Each employee can spend up to $2,000 to rectify a Customer relation issue. How are your employees empowered?

The sad truth is that most employees are not empowered by the companies that they represent. They have little power to change things or improve the company. Companies were often established using the top-down approach, so decisions do not get made anywhere close to the Customer. Many small businesses understand this problem and, at least as they mature, the business owner learns to empower their employees.

When I think about empowerment, I remember an experience that I had returning an item at a popular home store. We had the receipt and it had been purchased recently, so I assumed that this would be an easy transaction. We waited in line while the associate assisted another Customer. I found it odd when the manager had to come over to complete their transaction, causing the wait to be even longer. Finally, it was our turn. The cashier did the transaction and then asked us to wait so she could call over the manager to process the return to the credit card. Needless to say the manager was caught up doing other things and it took time and the line grew longer behind us. My reaction, which I voiced to the manager, was that if he was the only one who could approve returns, he should be the one to spend his day behind the service counter to process them.

In the service world we see this problem frequently. Decisions like this are made by people focusing on the wrong things and often have greater cost to the organization. If you ever have the chance, read *Linchpin* by Seth Godin. Seth's view is that we are still in the Industrial Age and workers are just cogs in the wheel. Everything is a process and we do our little bit for that process. According to Seth, we have two classes: the worker and the industrialist. When we leave, we are easily replaceable because of this process and class system. Seth then describes a new class, which he refers to as linchpins. This new class drifts between the industrialists and the workers and helps to guide the change the industrialists need.

Although I have a slightly different take on things, the end result is still the same. For example, I do not feel that the service world has always been this way. I refer to the past 20 to 30 years as the Jack Welch Era. Jack was the former CEO of General Electric. He popularized the use of the Six Sigma process, an improvement process started by others, most notably Motorola. Once Jack had rolled this out in the mid-1990s, other CEOs immediately began to follow. The basic premise of Six Sigma is that everything is measurable. These measurements guide the direction, not gut instinct. When you do a Six Sigma project everything is mapped and measured. Through this, you take out components that are guided by the metrics. As I started doing Six Sigma-based projects, I noticed that people were choosing measurements that told the story that they wanted to tell. This led me to believe that there are many business leaders who do want to run things like the industrialists, but most employees prefer to be a little more artistic and have some control. They want to guide their company's improvement and will work around the rules to do so. This is something that happens every day in our metrics-driven environment, but maybe it is time we found ways to allow this to happen in the open.

So what happens in call centers when process gets in the way? First, a good employee wants to do the right thing for the Customer as well as the company. The two can go together! Employees will first try to find legitimate ways around obstacles. I remember when I first joined Advanta, they had criteria for allowing fee waivers, but it did require certain things to be said by the Customer. The first time I heard it, I could not believe how silly it was. But agents are inventive! They would guide the conversation so it would meet the criteria and allow them to waive the fee. Of course the Customer was frustrated because it was not always easy for them to guess the magic words. My favorite instance was an agent who responded to the Customer, "What I hear you saying is that you will close the account if the fee is not waived, and I want you to know there is no need to do that because I have taken care of that for you." The Customer never said anything like that but the agent wanted to meet the rule just in case someone was listening. Needless to say, I told him that I did not care what the rule says; he should do the right thing, as he did. Trying to force the conversation into a rule was just poor management. Having a Customer on the other end of the line can be a difficult for anyone, especially if rules get in the way. Over the years working in call centers, my teams and I have studied interactions that resulted in disciplinary actions as a result of rules getting in the way. (Hopefully, you have never had a call that would require someone to receive a warning or be terminated, but it does happen.) We would focus on the entire interaction, not the specific portion that caused the disciplinary problem. We were surprised to learn that many of the interactions were on topics that agents had no authority to change. They were "it is what it is" moments usually involving decisions that could not be changed based on policy. The problem was that in many cases the agents were right to be frustrated. They had no good answer to provide to the Customer and the Customers were aggravated by their overall experience. We now had the ability to drive change and we did!

The Customer Service world is often driven based on two main thoughts: The employee is not able to be trusted and the Customer is trying to get one over on us. We have all been in situations where rules were created for the many due to the actions of a select few. This is often done in business, especially within Customer Service. What kind of message do these rules send? How do they make you feel? Well in the new world in which we live, this becomes our brand image. It is time to change.

CHAPTER
6

The Social Media Hype

Social media has been entirely overhyped in recent years. If you listen to many of the talking heads, they'll tell you to have your Facebook fan page updated, while tweeting and YouTubeing, all while providing a +1 and "Like" to everything you do. Social marketers are beating down your door, enticing you with Likes galore and more friends and fans than you could possibly know what to do with. It can get to be really old, really fast if you listen to all those talking heads. Don't get me wrong; I think that social media is changing the world in more ways than we can imagine, but the magic is not as euphoric as some will lead you to believe. Businesses big and small are having salespeople from marketing firms or places like Groupon, Facebook, LinkedIn, Foursquare, and many others promising monumental returns based on ads. Marketing agencies are proposing online gimmicks that will make your message spread across the web like wildfire. It will be the next viral hit! I am sure some of it is not doing any harm, but the question remains, "Is it worth the cost?"

You will have to answer this for yourself. If you are on Facebook, what are your interactions with brands like? If you tweet, how often do you have conversations with brands? I am in the business, and I will tell you that I do not have them very often. I personally prefer to use the spaces to interact with people. Human connections are the most important to me. Through those human connections, I may hear about brands, such as someone mentioning that they are buying something, or an experience that they had with a company, but these statements are not very frequent compared to personal updates from family and friends.

Social media is any place where discussions are happening online. It is that easy and it is that big. Facebook is a site where you connect with people you already know; I like to refer to it as your living room in that it is comprised of people and businesses that you would most likely invite into your living room. Twitter on the other hand is the site to meet new people. The real key to Twitter is search. If you want to find people talking about a certain topic, you can use Twitter search to locate the conversations and connect with them. It is really that simple. Not using Twitter or Facebook does not mean you avoid all social media or that you are not involved in social media. You may watch videos, talk in forums (or just linger), or maybe you just read reviews on consumer websites, like Amazon. These are all social media and where some of the greatest impact is happening. Before I buy a product, I usually find myself on Amazon to at least read reviews that Customers have left. Most people tend not to think of Amazon as a social media website, but for me it is a huge shift. Do you ever read reviews prior to making purchases? I know that I do. I also read reviews on Yelp, Angie's List, and many other websites. These are all channels that can perpetuate brand culture and advocacy.

Prior to the creation of review websites, a brand tightly controlled much of their message through advertising, PR, and other initiatives. We had word of mouth but it was limited to our close circle of friends, family, and coworkers. Today views can be rapidly spread to many more people with the click of a button. This has caused a lot of frustration for large and small businesses. There have been cases of competitors purposely writing negative reviews regarding the competition while writing positive reviews for their own business. Dishonesty happens and it can be very damaging.

The best way to combat any negative reviews is by creating the right experience for other Customers. For example, in the past, many hotels were steering clear of review websites like Trip Advisor, but today they are starting to encourage it. Why? By not encouraging it, the only people who would be likely to write a review were people who had a bad experience to report. By encouraging everyone to write a review, the good reviews may dilute the negative ones. Some good reviews will float to the top. This is one easy way to win in a hyperconnected world. Do not discourage reviews, but instead encourage your Customers to write them. The fact is that you would not be in business unless the vast majority of your Customers enjoyed their experiences with you. For some reason, human nature causes us to spread negative experiences, but when someone asks us to do something, we also feel obligated to do so if they delivered on our expectations.

You will notice that many of the ways to succeed using social media are common sense and psychologically driven, but surprisingly, most companies do not follow the easy path. When something is new, such as social media, or when the Internet gained popularity in the mid-1990s, experts come out of the woodwork trying to sell unknowing people all kinds of services. It does not matter if you are a small business or a large one, do not fall for all the hype. The first rule that I use when talking to salespeople is to ask, "As a Customer, would I care?" When these firms are selling to you, be sure to always thoroughly review recent examples of their work. The nice part is that their work should be in the public domain, so you should be able to easily view it yourself. Many of the promises that they offer will be more fans or Likes on Facebook or followers via Twitter. Do you know if a fan or follower is a Customer or prospective Customer? Are they even a human being? Oftentimes this cannot be answered with certainty.

One common misconception is that fans on Facebook will help your organization spread your message, especially because they will see all your wall posts. This is a myth. The way Facebook displays content depends on how engaged your audience is. If you have a large number of fans, and individual posts do not have engagement by your fans, such as "Like"ing the post or adding their comments, fewer people (as a percentage of your fan base) will see it as part of their newsfeed. Then, even if it is part of the newsfeed, many still will not see it based on the way they use Facebook. Users of Facebook, similar to Twitter, may not be logging in every day, and when they do, they may view only the first page or two of the newsfeed, so if the post was not within that timeframe, they have no hope of seeing it. Of course, Facebook will allow you to buy ads focusing on the content, but how often do you interact with ads on Facebook?

If you decide to have a Facebook fan page, knowing how content spreads (or doesn't) can help guide the content you create for it. The content should focus more on the interests of your users, as opposed to the business. This makes it more likely that they will share the content, and your brand will be a part of it. The key is creating the experience that causes your Customer to want to talk about your brand in a positive manner. One strong practice, if you are in a business that is not restricted, is sharing information from your fans. Congratulate them on their individual successes, even if they did not have their success because of you!

Geolocation is another hot topic in social media today. You may not have heard the term before but you most likely have seen it in action. *Geolocation* is using location-based technology to check in at places or to classify your current location where you are making a post. The most popular is probably Foursquare, but it is also common as part of Facebook status updates and tweets. Statistically, these types of services are used by younger generations to share current location with their family and friends. For the user it allows their friends to find them. For marketers, the information can be very powerful to know where your Customer is. As you can imagine this has created a lot of excitement and hype. It will be interesting to see how these services will be used long-term. I can understand why younger generations would use these tools: to meet up with friends wherever they are. At the same time, as they get older, will they want to share this information as freely? Don't necessarily follow the hype of today, but know your own Customer, what they would want to do, and whether geolocational services would be beneficial. The key is meeting their needs no matter where they are using tools they prefer.

I do find all the hype of social media alarming because it also means that many could be taken advantage of. During the Internet boom, people were buying all kinds of stocks and valuations for these companies that were not within their means. Often the companies did not even have profits. We have been seeing some of that within social media as well, although not to the same extent as before. There is a widespread belief that businesses have to be on Twitter and Facebook these days in order to compete. Many of your most passionate employees will share this belief. I have a friend who owns a franchiselike business. In the minds of their Customers, his company is clearly part of the larger organization. Some of his employees want to directly represent his business on Twitter and Facebook, but he is leery of it. He sees challenges and risks because there could be friction with the franchisor or other authorities in that field if the wrong message is sent out. In addition, he does not have the time or the energy to add this to his workload.

As we talked through it, it was easy to see that the franchisor already had Twitter and Facebook covered and that they are also staffed properly to handle the discussion in an appropriate manner and a timely fashion to ensure that the brand did not have a negative impact. For this business, the work of the franchisor was more than sufficient to meet the needs of his Customers without creating a negative impact for the brand, and it did not require the extra help from his own employees. He strongly encourages his team to support and participate in the franchisor's Twitter and Facebook efforts. He feels that this is sufficient to support the needs of his business and the needs of his employees, while avoiding duplication of effort. Assuming that all businesses should be on Twitter and Facebook is erroneous.

This hype does not mean you should or shouldn't be a part of this, and over the course of the book you will see where we are heading, how you can participate, and how your business will win. Here are some key ways to think about the social web:

- Relationship Building/Human Connections
- The Consumer Spreading the Message for Your Brand
- The Value of Information
- Passion

7

The Starting Point

When we think about social media, many people emphasize listening to Customers first. Sometimes it can be annoying to hear that over and over again, but to be honest, I am in that camp, too. I see a few key victories for businesses in the social world, and the first is the many insights that you can glean from listening to the discussions online.

If you are uncertain of the importance, let's take a deeper look at the Kotkin Enterprises case study mentioned earlier. It is easy to see how a blowup like the one on Penny Arcade can occur. Even without an active listening strategy, someone would have noticed the online discussion and told key business leaders, but what would have happened if you had been aware months earlier? The ideal scenario would have been to know these things before anything ever happened. Unfortunately, reviewing all correspondence can be difficult, tedious, and time-consuming. Even if you hired the right people, reviewing everything would be a waste of time. However, listening to Customers online is a vital way to improve your business.

To emphasize my point, what really perplexed me about the Kotkin example is that the same scenario had played out six months prior with Nate Stansell. You have not heard of Nate? Well, neither had I until I researched this. Nate is a Customer, very similar to Dave. He, too, had an experience like Dave's, and he chose to post the e-mail exchanges online for the world to see. Nate had ordered the Avenger controller in February. A few days later he received an e-mail saying that the controllers were sold out, but that he would be receiving an additional controller for free when the next shipment arrived. Later that month, Nate sent an e-mail again, inquiring about the status of his order. He was informed that the item was now scheduled to ship the following month. After the next estimated shipping day passed, Nate received another e-mail, explaining that the date had now been moved to yet the following month. When the next shipping day came near, Nate again e-mailed the company regarding the status of his order. This time, Nate was informed that there would be another delay and that the item would ship toward the end of the month.

This continued into the next month with a few phone exchanges on the same topic. Finally in mid-May, the item actually shipped. Nate ultimately received the product and it worked.

At this point, the only thing outstanding was the missing code to receive the second controller free of charge, as promised to Nate in the original delay e-mail from the company. Nate's frustration with the company was exacerbated, as he was forced to leave a phone message regarding the code. Nate's call prompted a return call from Kotkin's marketer, who had recently come on board as the marketing firm and support person. This is the same person who had been involved in the conversations with Dave in the earlier example. During their phone conversation, the obviously overwhelmed marketer let Nate know that he would follow up regarding the promised free controller. A few days later, Nate again followed up with an e-mail and from there, things spiraled out of control. At first, the marketer forgot the original phone conversation and assumed that this was a new inquiry regarding an order, so he responded by looking for the address. After stating that the company already had his address, Nate wrote about his poor service experience and clarified his position regarding the promised second controller. He demanded a thirty-day time frame for resolution or he would consider small claims courts. This evoked a very cryptic, downright odd response from the marketer. The marketer first scolded the Customer for demanding a free controller. My favorite quote from this exchange is "I'm the President of my company not The Avengers so keep your punk smite ignorant comments to yourself. If I wasn't trying to help you I wouldn't have e-mailed you back. Customer Service of old is gone; we're in a new generation now."

Well, the marketer is right. We are in a new world of Customer Service, but maybe not the way he is seeing it! You can guess that this highly unprofessional response from the marketer led to a new chain of e-mails. At one point the marketer, e-mailing in response to Nate's threat to share the entire e-mail exchange with the world on his blog, responded, "Post this wherever you want; you're one little person out of millions; we don't mind the attention negative or positive it's attention press and media for free; stir it up." Well, Nate did exactly that, and this is now part of the brand for the Avenger and Kotkin Enterprises.

Getting started on listening is something that you have probably already done. To enhance listening skills on the web, the first thing that business owners should think about doing is setting up a Google Alert for their business name. If you have already done this, I want to applaud you. If you haven't yet set up Google Alerts for your business, I strongly encourage you to put down this book and set up your Google Alerts immediately! I have several Google Alerts set up, including my name, businesses that I have worked for, and other topics that I am passionate about. It helps me stay connected and relevant. Google Alerts do not always provide the full spectrum of the discussion on the web, so there are a few other steps to take, but they are all just as easy.

With all the information that is at our fingertips, the challenge is getting to the info that is relevant to us. You want information that relates directly and significantly to the matter at hand. Google search makes it easy to find any topic that you deem useful, especially subject matter regarding your brand. Of course, if your brand includes common terms, the search may be more difficult. The first step in using Google search is building a search string that gets to the information that you are looking for. First, start with your brand. Then use advanced search to add terms or subtract terms that help narrow the results to include just posts that are important to you. Once you do that, you can use the date range to find more recent information. You then should repeat the search on Twitter, Facebook, and LinkedIn. Now to get more advanced, try to locate conversations that are important to your business, such as competitors and topics of interest.

There are tools that could make this easier, but there is a cost, so focusing on free tools is a crucial first step for any brand. Even if you work for a larger organization, implementing the same techniques can help you stay connected on topics that are most pertinent to your organization at that time. You will have a better idea of what you are looking for and want to see once you have started searching and reviewing results. I was doing these searches years ago when I worked for Vanguard Investments. It helped me learn from Customers talking about the brand, but it also kept me up-to-date on pertinent topics. It was not my job but it gave me an advantage that enabled me to move forward. Your most passionate employees already know where Customer discussions are happening, so ask them! Back in my Vanguard days, Morningstar hosted a forum (and still does) called Bogleheads Unite, a tribute to the founder of Vanguard, Jack Bogle. They were some of the most passionate people for the Vanguard brand and they helped many with their investment decisions. Beyond all that, they were also very well versed on the workings of Vanguard and the philosophy of the company. As a simple Customer Service employee, reading the posts helped to educate me. They also helped me formulate responses to Customers in a way they could understand. Just being a fly on the wall added value for me, and I am sure that many others benefit from their observations.

After developing an understanding of your own brand, focus searches on competitors and on topics that your Customers find most important. The easiest way to do this is talking directly to your Customers, your service employees, and your sales professionals. They can tell you what your Customers' passions are. By doing these searches you and your team will be able to better connect with your Customers. You will possess information that will help you strengthen your business position.

At some point, you may want to take it to another level by using a listening tool, like Radian 6, Visible Technology, or many others. First, determine if you would like to do the searches yourself, or hire a firm like NM Incite, a Nielsen McKinsey company, to do the searches for you. The downside to some of these tools is that they do not always have the same speed of information that is available for free through searching Google or the social websites themselves. This can also be an expensive undertaking. However, if you do find a lot of conversations, the tools can be used to help you manage the dialogue and better have your team participate in them. Firms that do the searches for you, often also offer advisory services to assist in times of crisis. They often excel at finding alternative searches for you. Even with the alluring benefits they offer, do not allow anyone to rush you into these purchases.

CHAPTER

8

The Snarky Web

I often find myself in conversations with people who have been jaded by the negativity that they have found on the web, and often refer to it as the "snarky web." Usually these conversations are driven by their experience with consumer review websites, complaint sites, or other items that they found while searching the web. These sites are a natural evolution tied to the experiences that Customers have had with companies they have done business with. After having limited say, Customers now have their turn to broadcast their thoughts.

One of the best examples of this is a website called the Consumerist. The website was founded by Gawker Media in 2005 to discuss consumer experiences. Since that time, they have opened the door to a variety of conversations about various companies. Among my favorites is the grocery store shrink ray. One of my local grocery stores, an independently owned franchise, still has old-fashioned signs for different products. One of the signs is in the ice cream section advertising "HALF GALLON ICE CREAM." When is the last time you saw half gallons of ice cream? First, ice cream companies went down to 1.75 gallons, then some tried to go to 1.5 gallons. It now seems to be coming back up, but the only place that I have seen half gallons has been at a local ice cream shop that makes and packages their own ice cream. The Consumerist highlights this type of faulty advertising.

Some of the stories that they post seem outlandish, especially Consumer complaints about their experiences. Over the years, I have helped Customers resolve complaints that they filed on the Consumerist regarding companies that I have worked for. Often, I would read the complaint and think that this could never have happened; yet inevitably, the Consumerist's reports prove to be accurate. I do not know how they sort through the thousands of e-mails they receive, but the ones they choose, no matter how outrageous, really have occurred.

Have you ever sent an e-mail to a CEO or other company executive? Figuring out e-mail addresses is not that difficult. First, Google the company name with the word e-mail and you will most likely find an e-mail for someone within the company. Once you know that, you can easily identify the structure a company uses for e-mail such as:

- jsmith@company.com
- johnsmith@company.com
- john.smith@company.com
- john_smith@company.com

This alone has changed the Customer Service field, because now it is easy for a Customer to directly share an experience with company leaders. Some of the most dreaded e-mails I have seen the word from company leaders came as a result of Customer e-mails. Now, I have never met a CEO who wanted to create poor experiences and they take very personally the bad experiences created by their company.

The Consumerist took this newfound power of the Customer many notches higher. Several years back, they started to popularize the e-mail carpet bomb. Users helped them post known e-mail addresses within specific companies. They would list these addresses and recommend sending your complaint to all of them, so that the complaint would reach many corporate leaders at the same time, dramatically increasing the chances of action being taken by the company. I do want to be clear that the Consumerist does not advocate doing this for first contact. In fact, they recommend exhausting normal channels first, and if that fails, to utilize an e-mail carpet bomb in order to be heard. Today when you try to Google "e-mail address for some larger companies," you will find your way to the Consumerist website very quickly and soon you are on your way to resolution. The Customer is gaining power and websites like the Consumerist have helped to facilitate this.

In 2007 the Consumerist started a contest unlike any other contest on the web. It is structured similar to the NCAA Tournament, but instead of playing for best team, the winner is considered to be the Worst Company in America. The first year, the winner was the Recording Industry Association of America (RIAA). I would guess that this was greatly influenced by the RIAA stance on pirating music. The runner up that year was Haliburton.

In later years, the winners were Countrywide Financial, AIG, Comcast, and British Petroleum. I have my personal views, but you have to agree that in the court of public opinion, these companies were seen in a very negative light during the years in which they were the big winner. By the way, the winning company receives some nice publicity for their brand and the Golden Poo Award.

Even I am a little shocked that I just wrote *golden poo* in this book, but the award has been going mainstream, as has the

Consumerist. What surprises me even more is that the Golden Poo Award, as well as the Consumerist, are now assets of another iconic brand, *Consumer Reports*. In 2008, Gawker Media sold the Consumerist to Consumers Union. Since that time, the reporting appears to be just as critical and snarky as it always was. The only difference that I have seen is that the ads are no longer paid and that they do share some content from the parent organization. I have also noticed that they have done more interviews with mainstream personalities, such as politicians and regulators. Many would say that this purchase was made to gain access to a broader reach and younger demographic than traditionally held by *Consumer Reports*. Although I tend to agree with that assessment, I would point out that in the press release, Consumers Union pointed to the growth that *Consumer Reports* was having, even as other publications were struggling. No matter what, the snarky web continues to go mainstream.

The web is filled with consumer complaint websites like the Pissed Customer, My 3 Cents, Planet Feedback, Get Satisfaction, and thousands of others. Even in the earliest days of the web, there were huge numbers of complaints in forums, newsgroups, and other spaces, even if they had not been organized for this effort. This to me was the natural swing. The old adage "a happy Customer tells two friends while an angry Customer tells ten" has always been somewhat accurate, and the Internet has allowed the audience for rants and complaints to expand exponentially. I am sure that the numbers have never been mathematically projected, but psychologically we do want to tell others when we have had a bad experience and we always have. The web just allows greater ease in doing that, as it is relatively effortless to post a complaint. For years, companies have marketed to us, advertising their first-rate products and services. They even tell us why we need these things. Let's face facts: These ads do not always live up to the expectations that they create. This generates displeasure and anger; we want to tell everyone how fictitious the ads are. Beyond this, we also have our own personal expectations. This is especially true of things that we are passionate about. For me, that tends to be technology, but for you it could be another passion. I build up my expectations regarding many new products, sometimes even before there has been any release of information by the company. When the product finally does come out, I tend to be very vocal about what it might be missing, even though I had no reason to expect it in the first place. We see this frequently with product announcements from companies like Apple, Hewlett-Packard, Samsung, and many others.

We discuss passion to a great extent in upcoming chapters, but the key learning here is that failed expectations do create vocal Customers. How do we mold the right expectations?

9

Scalable Intimacy

The human element exists in everything we do. Human connections and friendships are influential and part of every decision we make. Many in the business world think that we have taken the human element out and made it all about process or metrics; this is false. Trust is a big component in the social world and very difficult for brands to earn. The reason is that we tend to trust people, not logos. This human element comes out in the best of Customer experiences and also on the social web.

When you are dealing with a company's Customer Service team, or representative, or even a waiter or waitress at your local diner, what experiences do you remember? Was it the experience that was efficient and delivered exactly what you wanted? Usually it was that waitress or waiter who connected with your family, made a nice comment, or played with the kids. If you are speaking to a service representative and small talk led to a connection, you tend to remember that as well. Unfortunately, due to many reasons, personal connections are often hard to come by when dealing with Customer Service. Hopefully, the lessons in this book can help change that!

Within social media, the human element plays a colossal role. Radian 6, a Salesforce.com company, is a leader in the social listening space and is a listening tool for the social web. When I first started working with them I did not even know what Radian 6 was. My first interactions were via Twitter with their head of marketing, David Alston (@DavidAlston). David and I had many Twitter conversations about social media, where things were headed, and Customer Relationship Management (CRM). I knew from David's bio that he was the CMO for Radian 6 and that he liked to discuss listening, engagement, and CRM along with other interests such as Johnny Cash. David and I talked about social Customer Service and the astronomical power of listening. We did not always agree on topics, but they were always valuable discussions to me and I have a tremendous respect for David.

At the time Radian 6 was relatively new to the market and not the leader that they are today. They were building the next generation of cloud-based listening tools. When the time came to select a tool for our social listening efforts, we brought in the top companies, including Radian 6. We reviewed the capabilities of each and narrowed our choices down to our top three, of which Radian 6 was one. When we compared the top three, price was comparable and so were the features, but some of the tools were not fully cloud-based. We decided to go with Radian 6 partially because of my relationship with David. I always knew if I had a problem I could go to David for help. I trust him.

Personal relationships have always played a role in business. A friend and marketer from the Philadelphia area, Beth Harte (@BethHarte), uses a picture of a golf course when describing Twitter. Her point is that human relationships are always part of business, just like that executive golf outing. Social media brings a scalable intimacy to our interactions.

So what is scalable intimacy? I know that many marketers have focused on pushing a message out, but scalable intimacy, as demonstrated by David Alston, offers tremendous value. It is the ability of a company or employees of a company to create a personal connection with their Customers. Scalable intimacy is an important way to succeed in the social media realm. At this time, numerous businesses are not trusted, but they have employees who are trusted. These important assets should be utilized. Do you empower your employees to be themselves in social media? You should! Are you scared of your employees being themselves and discussing your brand? If so, you may not have hired the right people.

Most companies that I have worked for have blocked access to many social media websites, and I am sure that you have experienced the same. The concern, of course, is not as much about the brand, but over the fear that people will not be as productive because they have access to the social web, and that employees will spend their time talking to friends instead of working productively. Of course, this is probably a bit shortsighted. The fact is that smartphones, tablets, and other devices are making access to the web easy, instant, and right at your fingertips. So, is blocking websites effective or causing employees to use alternative means to get to the same result? Sometimes taking a more progressive approach can win over many. By blocking the websites, you are automatically telling employees that you do not trust them. How would you feel if someone told you that you are not trustworthy? The fact is that you might be able to leverage your employees and in the process increase trust and build the brand.

Zappos is almost always held up as an example of a company doing it right in social media, but that really comes down to their values. Tony Hsieh, Zappos' CEO, discusses their culture in his book *Delivering Happiness*. I will not fully outline it here, but I recommend reading the book to learn more about the unique culture that they have built. You can also visit their website. For Zappos it is all about living these values:

- Deliver WOW Through Service
- Embrace and Drive Change
- Create Fun and a Little Weirdness
- Be Adventurous, Creative, and Open-Minded
- Pursue Growth and Learning
- Build Open and Honest Relationships with Communication
- Build a Positive Team and Family Spirit
- Do More with Less
- Be Passionate and Determined
- Be Humble

Tony and his team have lived up to these values in everything that they do. It is obvious that they strive to hire the right people, who live by these values already. Beyond that, they educate their team on social media and encourage their employees to utilize it. Through this they are constantly building trust. This can be seen in action through social media, but also at events with their team members. One of the best examples of their employees living these values came during a difficult time, a time when many companies completely forget about the values they try to live up to. On November 6, 2008, Zappos had a layoff impacting 8 percent of their workforce. Tony was so open about the layoff that he even shared his internal e-mail with the world. Team members asked if they could even speak about the layoff in social media. They were not only allowed to talk about the layoff in social media, they were encouraged to talk about it.

Astonishingly, people who were laid off were commenting about how lucky they were to have had their time at Zappos. The accolades went on for days from those within Zappos, and more importantly, those not directly related to Zappos. If you had been laid off, would you want to praise your former employer? Many companies talk about values, but they are actually embedded in the culture at Zappos.

The story is much bigger than this one day for Zappos. It is really about the aura created by the company and the trust that the Zappos team has created with the world. This trust plays out every day when someone purchases a pair of shoes or any of the thousands of other items available. People have built up a loyalty to the brand. Many Customers are willing to pay more because of this trust and choose to do so every day. Tony and the team built this and as they have grown as a company, they have worked to continue demonstrating the values. Do you know anyone who shops at Zappos? Ask them how they feel about the brand.

We are in a world that is hyperconnected. Whether we want them to, or not, Customers and our competitors can catch a glimpse into the real internal culture of our business. This is because our employees represent the business. If employees are quiet in social media about their work, this silence sends a message that is almost as bad as the employee who trashes the company in social media. Is your employee an advocate for your brand? The fact remains that most employees are proud of the company they work for or the industry they are in. The key is tapping into that passion and encouraging them to share their deep affection. If you look around, many of your employees are already talking about their time spent at work. What are they saying? How is that reflecting on your brand? Are you creating the right experience for your employees?

When hiring in the Customer Service world, I have always found that passionate people, especially those passionate for the Customer, are the best people to hire. Later in the book I discuss this further, but you know the type that I am talking about! The person jumping up and down, offended that the company is doing something wrong for the Customer. Many service leaders dislike them, or at the very least are annoyed by them, because they can be difficult to manage, but let's face facts: It is impossible to teach passion, but you can easily help them guide their passion in the right direction. Mold their passion and use it to your advantage. Highly passionate employees often prove to be the best brand ambassadors.

The same practice holds true in social media. The space tends to recognize highly passionate people. Most small business owners are highly passionate for their business, so they do really well when they go into social media. Encourage your employees to live their passion. Teach them what they can and cannot share via social media. Enlighten them by stressing the benefits to their personal lives. At the same time if they do not have the desire to participate in social media, do not force it. It has to be something that they want to do for themselves. Forcing them to do something like this would have a very negative impact for the brand.

Here are a few ways that employees can participate in social media if they so choose:

- LinkedIn—Employees can benefit in building connections through LinkedIn to coworkers, Customers, and friends. In this space they can share their expertise and participate in groups that match their interests. This benefits employees because it helps with their long-term career objectives and introduces them to engaging people within their field. The employer gains because these connections can be used for sales, name recognition, and introductions to others that can be influential for your business. The fear that companies have is that this space is often used for recruiting, and there may be fear that someone could poach your employee. This could happen, but it could also easily happen without the business benefitting. Many employees are already there, so work with them.

- Twitter—I mentioned earlier that the biggest benefit to Twitter is connecting with people whom you do not know, which can be very beneficial for your employee. They can easily search to identify people and conversations that they are most interested in. For the business, the employee is building trust with many people, including existing and potential Customers. Think about the Radian 6 example with @DavidAlston. Can this help your business?

- Facebook—Your team can share thoughts from their day with family and friends, expanding the trust that they have for the business, and increasing their willingness to recommend your business to their friends.

- Blogging—If your employee has a blog, teach her about what items she can share from the workday. If it is relevant to what she is writing about, she might be willing to share some of her insights. As with any of these means, the employee must be open about the relationship to the business. Blogging is a great way to build thought leadership and expand on a variety of topics.

- Participating in other conversations—Your employees may want to participate in existing conversations by leaving comments on blogs, sharing videos, or taking part in forum conversations connected to your business. This can help your employee learn from others in the field, but also identify him or her as a thought leader.

The key for employees is following a few simple guidelines:

- Be honest in terms of who exactly they are and what their relationship is to your business. There is an infamous example of an employee from Belkin posting fake reviews on

Amazon. In another example, the CEO of Whole Foods, John Mackey, was discovered posting stock information on Yahoo! message boards. According to the *New York Times*, Mr. Mackey, under the user name Rahodeb, posted comments praising Whole Foods, while making negative commentary regarding rival Wild Oats Markets.

- Do not disclose confidential information. This may seem like a no-brainer, but employees do not always know what is confidential. Try to take the time to teach them.

- Abide by regulations. If you are in a regulated industry, make sure that your employees know what they can and cannot share via social media. Simply being in a regulated industry does not mean that employees cannot say anything. They can and should say things, but they may need to be cautious of recommendations, so knowing exactly where the line is drawn is key. Also know your privacy policies because in some industries, saying that someone or a firm is a client is not permitted.

- Avoid taboo topics—Depending on the nature of your business, employees may want to avoid topics that could make your Customers uncomfortable. This could be politics, religion, gender, inappropriate language, or other items. Just think about how a Customer might react before posting things.

- Be nice!—This may seem to be common sense, but unfortunately it is not always. First, your employees are passionate for your company and may defend it too much when circumstances may not warrant it. In the Customer Service field, we see that all too often during calls that did not go according to plan. In social media it can be even broader. There is a famous example involving a PR executive who was visiting a major client, FedEx, at the FedEx corporate headquarters in Memphis. Upon arriving, the PR executive tweeted, "True confession but I'm in one of those towns where I scratch my head and say, 'I would die if I had to live here.'" Well, many of the FedEx executives do live in Memphis and in the same manner I feel about Philadelphia, they, too, were offended by these words.

Some of the guidelines may make you anxious or even frighten you, but remember that many of your employees are already using social media, so helping them avoid trouble is a benefit to you and them. As they participate they will build the scalable intimacy with your clients and therefore build your brand. The key is setting them up for this success.

10

Intimate Connections

Scalable intimacy goes much further than a few conversations and employees being themselves. Your Customers have access to more information than ever about your business. They are using it to make decisions each day, but how are you using it?

Do you remember when buying a car was a cat-and-mouse game? You did not have any information to work with in order to determine the price you were willing to pay. Recently I went shopping for a new vehicle, which resulted in two experiences worth sharing. I first went into a local Honda dealership to check out the Honda Ridgeline. In the past ten years I have used pricing information that I found online via CarsDirect.com as my guide to determining the right price. I have also purchased using the service. This time, due to the convenience of the dealer, I went directly to their showroom. I test-drove the vehicle and had a very pleasant conversation with the car salesman. I made it clear that I was just looking, but that if we decided to go forward,

I was easygoing but my expectations were not of the typical back and forth. I determined my pricing using CarsDirect and *Kelley Blue Book* for the trade. If they were not in line with that price, I would not be interested. Ultimately, I did not want to waste their time or mine. At the end of the test-drive, the salesman shared and tried to sell all of the unique ways in which they provide service to their Customers, including a free car wash whenever they wanted it and oil changes for the life of the car. The facilities were impressive, shiny, new, and beautiful. The salesman professed that this was not like other car dealerships. He clearly stated that service was their number one priority. This was intriguing and promising for someone like me to hear. Service wins repeat business and I know that I would return if they treated me right. After the test-drive, I concluded that I liked the car and wanted to pursue a purchase. After taking the family home I returned to the dealership to start what I hoped would be a painless process. I anticipated a positive buying experience since they proclaimed to be so focused on the service experience. Of course, hope can get bashed quickly in this world! We sat down at the desk to start going over the numbers. Have you ever noticed the fuzzy way dealers like to present numbers? I hate that! Most people look at the overall price, then at the overall trade value. In true fashion, they pulled out the same old-fashioned deal sheet and started presenting the numbers. The salesman had a "fantastic" deal for me after checking with his manager. The numbers were thousands of dollars higher than the CarsDirect pricing and the trade was off by at least a thousand, so I reminded him how I determined my price. Again it was back to his manager. This time the salesman came back with *the* deal for me. Now the deal sheet was marked with red marker instead of pen, but the bottom line still wasn't close. At this point, I grabbed my keys and left. The next day I did receive a number of follow-up e-mails, all basically spam. Among my favorites was an e-mail titled "A Personal Response from [REDACTED] Honda." Here is the content of that e-mail:

Hello Frank,

Welcome to [REDACTED] Honda. Our mission is to provide you with a unique experience, both in sales and service, and your complete satisfaction is our only priority.

We have a huge selection of New, Certified Pre-owned cars, Vans and SUV's in stock and available for immediate delivery. You will find the same great satisfaction within our Service Department.

Our Express service is open 7 days a week.

Included with every New and Certified Pre-owned purchase:

FREE Oil & Filter changes

FREE Unlimited Car Washes

FREE Service loaners & Shuttle service

To serve you best, we invite you to visit our dealership to meet with one of our Product Specialists.

I will call you to set up an appointment so that we may be prepared upon your arrival.

Once again, on behalf of the entire team at [REDACTED] Honda, I thank you for giving us the opportunity to exceed your expectations.

I look forward to meeting with you,

Michael

Certainly not a very personal e-mail! Timeliness is key and I had already been to the dealership! I did follow up with an e-mail to explain my reasoning for not choosing this dealer. Although I REDACTED the numbers and unimportant data, portions of that e-mail are worth sharing:

Thank-you for following up regarding my recent visit. As you may recall I walked out with little feedback. Between the vehicle and the cleanliness of the dealership I was tempted to purchase the Ridgeline without too much more research. As we started to talk numbers the experience shifted to typical cars sales BS. This made all the other 'extras' seem disingenuous. I know that was not the intent but my expectations were higher based on our conversations and the environment. I am not a fan of the deal sheet or the manner [in which] most car dealers present numbers. It brings about a lack of trust to me. I should also mention another piece of feedback. Today I received 6 e-mails in a row including this "personal" e-mail that was not very personal.

Overall I think you are a good sales guy that is really good at building rapport. You will have success. My expectations were simply higher leading to my disappointment. I hope this provides clarity regarding my reason for leaving.

Frank

I did receive a response to this e-mail, which stated:

Frank,

Thank you for returning the e-mail. I apologize you felt this way with your visit. If I can be any help with you in the future please let me know.

Thank you

Michael

Over the course of the next month I received additional sales e-mails, but none that would make me want to return. During my initial visit, I had presented information about me, which was ignored and, after sharing so much about service, the salesman made it clear that he was not listening to me or interested in providing service. Unfortunately for Honda, this experience turned me away from their cars because I no longer have any interest in returning to that specific dealership for service after that sales experience, even though the location was convenient and the facility itself was eloquent.

A month or two later I did purchase a vehicle. This time I worked through most of the numbers online. Amazingly I got an even better deal than I could imagine. The dealership was under construction and the sales team was working out of a trailer, but this had no impact on service whatsoever. They were courteous, professional, and respectful of my time. There was no fooling around, just a great experience from Burlington Chevrolet in New Jersey. I was so wowed by the ease of the transaction and the overall numbers that I have been raving about the experience to everyone. Don't be fooled by impressive facilities; superior service is only about people. Remember that your employees have the ability to connect with Customers. Your team can exceed expectations and create wow experiences when you empower them.

After the sale, the dealer continued to wow me with little things. For example, the salesman and I are now connected via Facebook. They were also kind enough to send a tin of cookies with a nice personal note, hoping that my kids might enjoy them. My favorite was a personal, handwritten note from the vice president of the dealership. It was not lengthy, it simply stated:

> Frank,
> We appreciate your kindness as well as the business.
> Enjoy driving your Avalanche this fall.
> Best Wishes,
> Gus

We do not receive handwritten notes often, so it was nice to see someone take the time. There is no doubt that I will be returning to that dealership in the future!

Information is key today, and the challenge is how to manage it all and how to utilize it effectively. Customer Relationship Management, or CRM, is a popular means for salespeople to manage their relationships. These tools help the best in class companies manage relationships effectively across each touch point. As more is learned about the Customer, it is collected in their repository for future reference. This is helping to scale intimacy, but it can now be raised to all new heights by incorporating social information. The term *Social CRM* has been gaining ground in the past few years. This has meant everything from social servicing to an add-on to existing CRM tools, to countless others definitions. My view is that Social CRM is a component to your already existing CRM. By connecting the information that you have already collected to the information available in social channels, you have a deeper understanding of your Customer.

As an example, a healthcare salesperson might collect information during each visit to a doctor's office. He knows each member of the staff and what is a driver for them at work. Maybe a few of the staff members post often—on Twitter and LinkedIn. By accessing this information, the salesperson now knows what these individuals want the world to know about them. Maybe on Twitter they discuss their hobbies and on LinkedIn they are having professional conversations about charitable efforts that they are involved in. Do you think that this information might be helpful during upcoming visits? Remember that the world is not all that different. We thrive on human connections and this information can help build them.

Information is an amazing relationship builder. We already know that LinkedIn connections of our friends and family can help us get introductions to key people who may influence our future. It does not matter if the introduction is career oriented or for meeting your sales quota. If you are connected to me and I know someone whom you are trying to meet, I can arrange that virtual connection for you. LinkedIn proudly shows us this when we log in. I have 1,246 connections as I write this. These connections link me to 12,352,679 people. Are you leveraging this across your employees? How about your Customers?

Now let's take it to a higher level. Those other examples are some of the easy ways that this information can be useful in building your business, but how about in the business to consumer space? For years, I have been hearing people interested in increasing their fan or follower count as a way to expand their social efforts. The funny thing is that very few companies can even identify if a fan or follower is an employee, Customer, prospective Customer, or even if they are human at all. I know that people love to have fans or followers but we have to keep it real in terms of exactly what this metric represents. I have been paying close attention, and I do think that people are starting to realize this and that in the coming years they will strive to better connect the dots. So what do I see businesses starting to do? Activities that connect your Facebook profile to the company will allow the business to know and understand their fan base better, so apps that have you provide your Facebook information to your account with the company will be much more prevalent. This will help the business better understand their audience. They can also more effectively measure their performance in social media because they will be able to see if it is helping to drive sales for those Customers or not. Of course that is only step one. As we start to better connect the social media information, we can also better understand what is important to that individual Customer. I often talk about technology-related things in my life, so imagine if the next advertisement that comes to me in the mail is geared specifically toward a topic that I am already interested in. That would be impactful to me and I might pay more attention to it than one that is generic. I am not one to pay close attention to any ad, so if you can get my attention, you could easily win a sale.

Now let's take this even further. Years ago, I worked on initiatives to send calls to Customer Service representatives who had similar interests to the Customer whom we were serving. Isn't that a novel approach? Instead of targeting based on relationships, we built off what we already knew worked well: human connections. Understandably, the challenge we experienced when we experimented with that was having a deep knowledge of the Customer, but now social media can help fill that gap. Scalable intimacy can now be taken offline and brought to other communications channels in many more exciting ways.

The major search engines are already planning to use social profiles to better provide search results to you based on your friends and conversation that you already had via Facebook, Twitter, Google+, and so on. This will be a game changer in terms of how we find information, or as Erik Qualman, author of *Socialnomics*, pointed out, at some point, we will not find the news; instead, the news will find us.

Are you freaked out yet and rushing to delete your social profiles?

Privacy will become an even larger concern in the future. The European Union has already started plans to make sure that information in social networks is not used improperly and that the control is within the hands of the users. With all of the privacy issues that Facebook has faced over the years, I wonder that if a new network came along that offered stronger privacy protection, would there be a mass exodus to that site?

Just like other communications methods, it is imperative that you establish guidelines for your business regarding how the information obtained from your Customers will be used and how individuals can opt out of sharing their information. There are many people who do not realize how public their information is via social networks or how easy it is to connect the dots to determine who they are. Companies that overuse the information or use it in a very big brother way will be punished. Those who use it properly with the right level of caution will win Customers through the connections that they are able to build.

Privacy concerns are abundant. For example, there is a lawsuit currently in court in California regarding Facebook's new product called Sponsored Stories. As you may already know, many of us avoid clicking on ads, unless it is something truly compelling. Facebook saw that, too, so in response, they created Sponsored Stories, where they show the activity of your friends with a particular brand. Seeing that your friend liked something makes it more compelling to you, too. Facebook was simply highlighting an activity that your friend was already doing, and profiting from the results. The lawsuit was originally dismissed based on the website's terms of use, but another judge on appeal has allowed the lawsuit to proceed. The outcome will be interesting to watch as well as the impact it may have for Facebook. How would you feel if you were featured in an ad? The ad simply says you liked something, which is the same thing that might appear in a timeline after you had taken the action. We will have to watch and see!

All this talk of information and privacy leads me to think about Klout, PeerIndex, and other similar tools. Klout and tools like it attempt to measure one's influence on the Internet. You may have heard of influencer marketing, which is the belief that by targeting people influential to others regarding your products and services, they in turn will spread the message. Well, how do you determine who is influential? Tools like Klout or PeerIndex are trying to measure exactly that. This is a topic for which you can usually find some very diverse views. If you create the right experience, others will take your message and carry it out for you. When I look across the web, the first thing that I notice is that strong content is what tends to spread, regardless of who created the content in the first place. One of the companies that I worked for had had a famous video go viral long before I started working there. Today more than 1.6 million people have viewed the video. The person who posted the video had posted only two videos ever, yet one of the two had very strong negative brand influence. The video has entertaining content for those who watched it, but not for what the brand is about. It is the good entertainment that drove the influence, not the brand's message.

About a year ago an influencer-marketing agency e-mailed me trying to solicit business. In the e-mail, they told the story of how they had distributed really cool kits to bloggers to get them to talk about an upcoming show premiering on a premium cable channel. I read the e-mail and immediately wrote back to say that I have been a paying subscriber of the channel for years and that, as one of their Customers, I was upset that I, too, had not received the package. The agency did immediately write back to offer me a kit, which I declined. I was trying to make a point. In their effort to get people to talk about the show, they had also been sending a not-so-positive message to others, specifically to the Customers for that channel.

In 2009, the Federal Trade Commission (FTC), based on a lot of activity on blogs, established a guide to testimonial advertisements, including bloggers and celebrity endorsements. Under the notice, those receiving compensation, including free products, must disclose this fact. Prior to that rule, there had been a free-for-all aspect to the net and endorsements. For example, I had been invited to a party where companies pay to come and give very expensive free products out to bloggers with the hope that the bloggers would then go and talk about the company or product in a positive light. Now, under these rules, the individual posting the review on a free product can be in trouble for not properly disclosing that fact, even on a short post like a tweet. The company can also get penalized if they know that something was not properly disclosed.

As I was writing this, I came across another interesting example. As a parent I can honestly say that all of my children have thoroughly enjoyed and learned from LeapFrog products. Over the years I have been impressed and, in general, I think the world of the company and greatly appreciate the many hours of entertainment and learning that they provide and continue to provide. We have countless LeapFrog products at home and I buy more and more every year for my own children and as gifts for other children. Today I was searching LeapFrog because they have a new product coming out called the LeapPad. I actually noticed it in some Target stores, so I went to the Target website to read some reviews. There are not many yet, but the six that are there were interesting to me. Many of them read like this one from "Parenting By Trial and Error" from Chelsea SD:

> I received the LeapPad to review for LeapFrog on various sites, as well as on my blog. Though I received the LeapPad for free, the opinions expressed here are my own. We have been using and loving LeapFrog products for years at our house. As I expected, my boys, [ ], love the new LeapPad. From the clear, kid-friendly touch screen to the easy-to-use camera and video recorder, they've been having a blast with it ever since it arrived. I love that it allows several children to create profiles so that the LeapPad can keep track of each child's progress and skill set. I also love that the games and apps are interchangeable with the Leapster Explorer. Of course, like all LeapFrog toys, the LeapPad is helping my kids learn AND have fun at the same time. [ ], and they are perfectly happy with their LeapFrog toys. I'm even happier than they are because they're not playing mind-numbing games. Way to go, LeapFrog!

It was at this point that I Googled reviews for LeapPad and found numerous examples. On some level, I now feel less valued by LeapPad in that they would give away free product to others. More importantly, I lost faith in every review written on the topic, as I am skeptical because the product was given away.

This type of thing has happened with books for years, so Amazon fought back. Many of their reviews now state if/when the review is associated with an actual purchase. Although reviews may seem all the rage, especially with social websites like Yelp or Amazon, there may be a coming backlash against some of them, especially ones done on a company website as opposed to a reseller, like Amazon, as there can be a higher chance of biased reviews on actual company websites. I read reviews frequently, and for the most part I can quickly tell which ones I trust and which reviews are useless. Trust in this information is key, and I am afraid that some will take this trust away. I applaud Amazon for adding the verified purchase information to their reviews.

Getting back to Klout, the company has tried to create a mathematical formula to provide a score that matches up to someone's online influence. Where I see the value here is learning more information, such as topics that influencers are most interested in. Klout scores fluctuate and influential areas change. At one point, Klout said that I was influential on Mary Poppins! My Klout score currently says that I am influential about social media, Customer Service, marketing, business, Citi, Technology, Amazon, Blogging, Job Search (not sure why), Klout (I find that funny), Media, Comcast, and Retail. That could be useful for someone to know about me. They even have a way to define one's style in social media. When I am writing this my style is *specialist*, defined by Klout as follows:

> You may not be a celebrity, but within your area of expertise your opinion is second to none. Your content is likely focused around a specific topic or industry with a focused, highly engaged audience.

At the time that I am writing, my Klout score is 58, but I tend to range dramatically based on how frequently I post. Sometimes I do not post as much, and my score drifts lower, while at other times it is much higher. I have ranged between 45 and 70.

There is a world of information out there, some good and some bad. If you are looking at things with your Consumer lenses, you may like that you can find information on virtually every product, making buying decisions easier, and allowing you to see the impact that some things, like reviews, have. You may also be concerned with what information you are putting out there for the world to have access to. From a business perspective, people are still trying to determine the best value for their business. To me, one of the keys is access to information, but that will last only as long as it is used in an appropriate fashion that does not cause concern for your Customers. Listen to your Customers carefully in everything that you do!

11

The Social Business

The next big catchphrase is "Social Business." You will most likely see all kinds of discussion on the topic and it is important enough that I feel the need to discuss it here. *Social business* is the culmination of much of what has been discussed so far regarding social listening, social CRM, and your employees' actions within social media. The other key component is the social workplace. There will be a shift in how we do business. Many of us are familiar with the command and control style of leadership, but that does not always make the most collaborative workforce.

The Millennial Generation is very different from Generation X or the baby boomers. The Baby Boomer Generation worked well with a top-down structure. Boomers waited for their time to take the reins and did an amazing job. Generation X did not always like that style but would still fall into line and do what was expected, according to their baby boomer bosses. Now that they are taking the reins, part of the mark that they leave will be a different leadership style. Adding to the shift in leadership, the Millennial Generation is becoming a dominant force in the workplace. I sometimes prefer to call this group Generation Why, because they like to question things, even the senior most leaders. They are not as much into hierarchy as were prior generations; they also tend to prefer group discussion. This is because they were brought up in a time when we were more connected than ever. They do not need an e-mail telling them what to do. They would respond better to a blog post with others presenting their thoughts as well. Oftentimes the actions of the Millennial Generation are mistaken as disrespectful when in reality they are simply trying to build a deeper understanding. The millennials are fiercely loyal to people, not companies. They are not afraid to share a differing view and they do not mind others challenging their thoughts. The challenge to you is how do you meet their needs in a business world that is currently designed very differently?

The Millennial Generation is very comfortable with social tools like Twitter or Facebook, and in many ways these tools help facilitate the way they think. Obviously most businesses cannot have their private conversations moved to the public forum, but bringing these style tools internally allows a company the ability to facilitate the dialogue that works for this important group of employees. This can be done easily with very inexpensive tools. Of course, the tools are not the problem; it is the internal trust component. If your employees do not trust the organization, or have a fear of retribution for things they say, implementing the tools will not bring success. Internal trust must be embedded in the culture.

One of the frustrations within service groups is that they do not always have the ability to influence change in their organization, but imagine if they were using an internal version of Twitter to talk to each other. Then, an executive could search through the data and see trends the moment they start. Product teams could be closer to the Customer than ever before. People around the globe could easily get to topics that are of interest, and some of the largest companies could gain a much more agile work force that is able to collaborate and avoid all the duplication that happens today.

Social media has connected people globally and the same can happen within your business. It does require a comfort level that shifts control from the command side to the organization. The key for the leader is making sure that the organization is focused on the right goals and a clear path. It comes down to having the right people on the job and trusting them. If you can accomplish this, you can lead the way.

Once you have started this, you are on the path to being a social business. It will require a different leadership style but the reward is the countless efficiencies that businesses have been looking for. Businesses that win at social business will be leading the way over the next five or ten years because they will be nimble enough to be able to bring in the right results. They will also be the employer of choice for many people. The world is driving dramatic change at an accelerated pace and this is one way to win in the new world order.

I do not profess to know the ins and outs on this topic, but there are many thought leaders in the space. Key people whom I like to pay attention to are Brian Solis, Charlene Li, and Peter Kim. Brian has many books that can be useful to reference, including his latest, *The End of Business As Usual*. Charlene wrote *Open Leadership* and Peter Kim has partnered with his colleague Dion Hinchcliffe to write *Social Business by Design*.

CHAPTER
12

Connecting

So what does all this talk of social media, the workforce, and data have to do with being @YourService? Times have already changed for the service world and this book serves as a guide to changing with those times. The formula for winning in the social web is actually easy:

$$CE \times P = SMS$$

Company Experience (Product + Customer Interactions + Employee Experience)
$\times$ Passion = Social Media Success (or Failure)

When we observe, review, and analyze discussions about companies, we find that people tend to talk about products that they love. They also tend to talk about products that fill a unique need. Keurig is a great example of a product that fills a unique need. There is a lot of online discussion about Keurig and countless recommendations, both online and through word of mouth. I first heard about it through my wife who had learned about it from a friend. The funny thing is the friend is not even a coffee drinker, but there are times when you need it in your house and she thought it was perfect!

As I mentioned earlier, one of the brands I love to talk about is Apple. As a company, they do not have many company sponsored social media activities, yet their products are discussed frequently. There are websites established by fans just to talk about Apple products. I visit MacRumors.com on a daily basis, as well as MacWorld.com and many more.

Another company that has seen great success in generating social discussion is Coke, but much of that success is not based on the activities of the company, but on the passion people have for their product. How do you tap into the passion of your Customers? Employees?

Although I am not a product person, I know the products that I love and what I like to talk about. The challenge that most product people have is that they view things through their own lenses as opposed to looking from the Customer's perspective. Does your Customer base have passion for your product? Will they have a view on the differences from competing products? Why would they want to buy your product? Why would they need your product? Why would they talk about it to their friends?

Now a vital part of generating this passion is the Customer experience. Today, the largest segment working in the Customer Service field is the Millennial Generation. They require us to rethink the experience they have as employees and tap into their strengths. Doing so will help change your organization and help energize passions that they have as well as improve the Customer interaction component for the formula previously mentioned.

The term *passion* can sometimes be misused and is often overused, especially within social media, but it is difficult to find a better descriptor. Dictionary.com defines *passion* as "any powerful or compelling emotion or feeling, as love or hate; strong amorous feeling or desire; love." As a Customer, what do you enjoy and feel comfortable sharing with your family and friends? I doubt that you share things you do not care about. Instead you share what you are passionate about, things you love, or things you hate. Obviously, passion can vary widely from individual to individual. Some are passionate shoppers, while others may be savers. As I mentioned, I am passionate about technology, coffee, and Customer Service. I like to live my passion in everything that I do, which includes talking about these topics within social media. In fact, I rarely talk about other things. This is the trend that most of us tend to demonstrate. What are the passions that you exude?

I have realized over the years that passion can be the driver of a lot of positive conversations, such as about Apple and Coke, but what about negative passion? How does that play a role? That leads me to the next major topic of conversation, Comcast. Whenever I mention Comcast to others, it tends to solicit a reaction, often negative. I was very open earlier in the book that when I joined Comcast, I reacted the same way. However, after spending a number of years within the organization, especially dealing with some of the toughest complaints, I have come to a few conclusions that may surprise you. Now, I am not going to say that I think that their Customer experience has been, or even is now, exactly what they would want it to be or what I would expect it to be. But they are continually striving to improve the Customer experience, and I know that they will be successful.

At the same time I have realized over the years that cable connects us to the world through TV, the Internet, and the phone. Cable and Internet are our lifeline in this hyperconnected world! It is an essential part of our daily routine that connects us to others. We get our information and news, talk to our friends, and so much more. We may not be as passionate about land-line phone service as we once were, but the Internet and TV are key to our connection. In fact, the Internet has become such a large part of our life that we are lost when it is not available. For example, after I had left Comcast I experienced an outage for a few hours. In retrospect, it was the first outage that I could remember in years. But I initially reacted in a negative manner, before catching myself from overreacting. In all fairness, I have had tremendous service with the only exception being electrical outages here and there, which they cannot control. When I look at companies cited on lists declaring poor Customer Service, often I see that same passion at play. We may not declare our love for the brand, but we do love being connected, which raises our own expectations to greater levels.

We all know that TV providers of all kinds have become infamous for their price increases, outages, fights with TV net-works, and all that. I also know that many people are constantly seeking alternative ways to feed their passion. In 2011, Netflix was a constant feature in the news because of the backlash they had received from their Customers regarding a price increase that had been imposed. Basically, Netflix planned to split their DVDs by mail service from their streaming service, which for many would result in an increase amounting to as much as 60 percent. Needless to say, the passion that people have for entertainment (and low prices!) came through loud and clear. I've always personally wondered how Netflix could make a profit at the low cost they were offering their services and the seemingly high cost of sending DVDs via the postal service. I am sure that the processing of each DVD had a cost impact and Customers with quick turnaround times would have tremendous costs in comparison to Customers with longer turnaround times. No matter their cost structure, the passion of their Customers came out loud and clear. Customers viewed Netflix as an alternative means to fulfill their passion for entertainment, but Netflix was raising their rates. Later, Netflix attempted to explain that they were creating a separate entity, Qwikster. Netflix would continue as the streaming business, while Qwikster was going to take on the DVD-by-mail business. This, too, created an uproar and eventually Netflix had to back down from creating the separate entity altogether. However, they did not back down from the price change and they have paid dearly for this decision, losing 800,000 subscribers and a plunge in their share price. (It should be noted in the following quarter, Netflix did gain 600,000 subscribers so it will be interesting to watch how that continues.) How we communicate to our Customers in this new world will have a deep impact on the way we do our business.

CHAPTER
13

The First Weeks at Comcast

When starting a new job, most people typically experience a honeymoon or transition period. This is the perfect time to build connections within an organization and increase your own understanding of how the business operates. Prior to my working at Comcast, a large portion of my career had been spent in the financial services realm, so this was a totally new experience for me. I underestimated the depth of the challenges that lay ahead. I joined Comcast's national Customer Service team to manage the executive complaint department. In the weeks leading to the job, my excitement about the possibilities of creating change in the organization and improving the overall performance for Comcast's Customers and shareholders grew. The organization was also growing tremendously and we were preparing to move to beautiful new headquarters in Center City, Philadelphia.

My own expectations waned substantially almost immediately after I started. I learned that the process that my team used was basically taking a message and forwarding this message to the field for handling. The crash course in Comcast operations was fast and furious. A few days after I started, my time listening to calls had to come to an end and immediate action was needed. Bob Garfield posted his blog post "Comcast Must Die" on Adage's website. We had to respond but quickly needed to figure out how. The field was working to correct the trouble that Bob was having. Our PR team wanted us to try to help those commenting in detail on the post and to try turning things around. Again, I underestimated the difficulty of the assignment. Unfortunately, blog comments do not include names and account numbers. Our only way to identify the Customers was to search multiple billing systems trying to find a match. This was even more troublesome because you had to know where Customers lived to pinpoint exactly where to search. The anonymous web was not making it easy for the team.

Thanks to the work of two team members, we were learning how to be digital detectives; we were identifying Customers, calling them, and turning things around. This was never going to be a feasible, long-term answer but it was the beginning to an amazing story. Bob continued on his quest to bring what he called a "jihad" to Comcast and drive change. Bob's efforts resembled something that is now referred to as "Dell Hell" when Jeff Jarvis and many Dell users started discussing their experiences with Dell years earlier. I would imagine that this served as inspiration and fueled the fire for Bob in his quest against Comcast. What does a company do when such an uprising happens?

Have you ever noticed that most companies do not make it easy to log a complaint against the organization? It seems fairly basic, but most companies simply send you back to the channel in which you already had the frustration with. One of the reasons why Customers are taking to the web to complain about your brand is because you are not giving them another means to share feedback with you. Often the trouble at companies is simply that service is broken up into components to make things easier within the company. In the cable industry this is often separated geographically, so depending on where you live, your experience with the company can be vastly different. This is not unlike companies that have separate servicing departments based on product, or a franchise model where the service experience can vary dramatically from one location to another. The trouble is that the Customer usually sees you as one brand and not the way that you have chosen to divide yourself. At Comcast it became apparent that we needed to provide our Customers with a mechanism to share their feedback directly with us, as opposed to venting randomly on the web.

As this was all unfolding and Bob Garfield was about to launch a stand alone blog dedicated to continuing his crusade, Comcast was working diligently to identify ways to improve. One of the first steps was bringing in a new leader to help unify the Comcast Customer experience. During my first month, one of the leaders who had enticed me to join Comcast was moved into a new role and a new player was about to enter the picture. Rick Germano was a longtime cable guy, well respected in the field for his ability to lead and drive change. It was absolutely the right move and he was probably the only person who could have gotten that ball rolling.

Before Rick came on board, we had had a team assembled to determine how we were going to deal with the latest social media issues for the organization. We knew that Bob Garfield was creating his standalone website and he had an audience that he could rally. The team consisted of PR, marketing, outside consultants, and our Customer Service team. The issues we were facing stemmed from the convergence of how service influences your brand, and it required a new level of cooperation to drive and facilitate change.

The first step we took was to review how Customers contacted us, especially on our web properties. We soon realized that this was a key pain point because like many other companies, we guided Customers to our lowest cost of service, even if it was not their preferred method or the right one for their issue. We quickly changed that by building a Contact Us page that provided options for every method of assistance. We made sure that links were prevalent on all of our web properties. If you needed help, we wanted to make sure that it was easy for you to get it. We then took it one step further; we made it easy for you to share your feedback with us by creating a program called "Ask Rick." Shortly after welcoming Rick to the team, we had to let him know that we already planned to post his picture on our website while working to collect Customer feedback. Welcome to the team!

Our "Ask Rick" link went live in mid-October, just in time for Bob Garfield's "Comcast Must Die" website to be launched. Immediately "Ask Rick" was inundated with feedback. Over the coming weeks we had to work hard to build a new process to handle the channel while simultaneously focusing on turning these Customer experiences into positive ones. Clearly it was better for us to go through our internal channels than have complaints posted online for the world to see. We were working around the clock trying to keep up with the volume. We were also trying to find the right ways to staff this new channel. My team, along with teams in the field, did an amazing job at keeping up on it and establishing the building blocks to improve the Customer experience. We knew that the best way to reduce the volume in the future was to create the right experience in the first place! Change takes time but we were on the right road!

The next aspect of the turnaround was meeting directly with Customers and employees. This task would fall on Rick's shoulders over the coming months, with a detailed plan to document his travels. We outlined the areas to visit, hitting most of the major markets that Comcast serves. In each area, Rick would meet with Customer Service employees and technicians to obtain their thoughts on the organization. He would then meet with Customers, especially the ones we have had feedback from. At the time Comcast did not have a blog, so we posted write-ups on our website about each visit, what we had learned, and thoughts about how the feedback would turn into action.

Rick has tremendous strength at bringing people to his views. His role was traditionally to help bring best practices to each region, building tools that can be used by all the areas, and guiding the overall direction. The challenge was that it relied on the local leaders, reporting into others, to buy in to ideas and implement the recommendations. The field recognized that Rick had the expertise of their business. The field respected him and trusted his recommendations. In these early days, we might not have had much success without Rick Germano and his extensive knowledge of Comcast and the cable industry.

While Rick was driving change, we still had to deal with the crisis set in motion by Bob's "Comcast Must Die" website. Even though we were offering alternative ways to contact us or escalate, Customers were still going to Bob's website to vent their frustrations publicly. Many companies tend to ignore these rants, especially on deeply negative sites like this one, but we took a different approach. At first we continued what we were doing on the original blog post; if we could identify the Customer, we would try to work things out for them. This led to posts like this one:

> After posting my open letter to Comcast executives on 11–27–07 in the Customer Disservice section of 'Comcast Must Die', I called Comcast Corporate in Philly, speaking with a secy, in the office of Rick Germano (Sr VP Customer Care). She took down all pertinent info and told me it would

be directed to the proper departments. Later that same evening I did receive a call from a hi level tech who was experienced in dealing with e-mail problems. I was still doubting his credibility after all the misinformation I previously had received from other techs. However, after 1–2 hours, much to my dismay, all of the e-mails that were blocked since 10–12–07 suddenly started to come into the inbox with the force of a phospho-soda laxative, literally hundreds. The following day I did receive 2 phone calls from Comcast Execs, Mr Eliason and Mr Spence who were apologetic and sympathetic for the situation and assured me that there are ongoing improve-ments being made in their Customer care service. I was gen-uinely impressed by Comcast's quick response to both my phone call and the posting on this blog, which seems to be required reading for Comcast Customer Care Dept execs. KUDOS!!!!!!!!

Sincerely,

Steve

It may seem odd to start getting kudos on websites like Bob Garfield's "Comcast Must Die," but they were there! Beyond that we were also better able to identify opportunities for improving the processes for our employees and our Customers. Change was in the air!

CHAPTER
14

What Is Your Customer Guarantee?

What is the guarantee that your business offers to your Customers? Whether expressly written or not, your Customers have an expectation of your company and in their mind, that is a guarantee. Sometimes that guarantee is dictated by the industry that you are in. The cable industry at the time may have looked to Customers something like this:

- Rates will go up as much as possible.
- Your call will be ignored.
- A tech visit will be between 12 and 12.
- There is nothing you can do about it because you are stuck with us.

I say that all facetiously, but in reality the perceptions about your brand drive what people assume are how you stand. When you read all the negative commentary you could come to the same conclusion. You can pick out numerous examples, like the Department of Motor Vehicles (DMV). I would guess that their guarantee might look something like this:

- Spend all day in line.
- Fill out lots of paperwork.
- Get sent out of line to later return.

I am sure that we could do a whole comedy routine on what brands or industries supposedly stand for. In some ways it would be funny, but at the same time it would be sad because there is always some basis in reality to it. Perceptions are realities to the person who has them. What are your Customers' perceptions?

Many brands have difficulty because their own marketing and PR messages do not always match the business realities of the Customer experience. These differing messages are part of what is leading to the existing Customer revolution that is taking place. For years Customers have felt they do not have a say in the way a company treats them. In addition they have felt that they had no way to provide that feedback to the business, or that the business will ever take action on their feedback. Today, Customers do have this ability. They just turn to social media to express their views or vent their frustrations about the company. In reality they now have the ability to take control of the message about your brand. They can quickly and easily spread their message to anyone who will listen.

At Comcast, we were working as a cohesive team to address these issues. We first recognized the opportunity to make it easier for Customers to communicate with us, and we made those changes. That was the easy part; we now had to embark on something much harder: creating real change with the Customer experience. The first key efforts were listening to what our Customers were telling us. Next, we had to find improved ways to respond to Customers and solve their problems. In an effort to do this we focused efforts on improving our online help forums. Many companies, like Comcast, have forums on their websites that allow Customers to help other Customers. This was something that we already offered, but we recognized that we had to further improve this experience in order to encourage more Customers to be a part of that community. We also wanted to be more transparent in our dialogue with our Customers and other key constituents, so we started working on building a Comcast blog.

The work to redesign our forum started immediately. We studied existing forums and we worked with our community members to find the best means to increase the number of Customers participating in the space. We focused on solutions for trouble, so Customers could easily find what they were looking for. We also changed how we managed it, moving components to a centralized team so that we could more efficiently disperse information found within the forums, but also so that we could effectively provide clear, updated information when necessary to become more transparent to our Customers.

We also began working to create a blog for the overall organization. Early in this process, we recognized that the strength of Comcast is the people within the organization, so we sought a way to present that to the world that demonstrated the diversity of the people, thoughts, and activities that make Comcast. The name "Comcast Voices" stems from that exact thought and to this day the blog continues a tradition started at a very different time for the company. Over the years the blog has provided the organization with the ability to share a little of the internal information, the changes that were happening, and the good that the organization has done in communities in which we served.

Over the years, the company, like the cable industry as a whole, has had a number of incidents that added to the perceptions of poor service. Each one of these incidents led to real change. The jokes about the typical time window for technician visits being ridiculously lengthy led to a completely different way of doing things called "dynamic dispatch." In the past, technicians were provided stacks of paper, each one representing a visit scheduled that day. The technicians would then travel to each in the order they were supplied. Of course, this meant that they were often traveling across towns multiple times a day or sitting in traffic. It also made it nearly impossible to accurately predict when your technician would arrive. Today this is done more dynamically so technicians are sent to places that make sense and are convenient. Unfortunately, there was also an infamous video of a technician placed on hold while waiting to speak with a Customer Service representative. That video led to new tools for technicians so that they would never need to call. Working smarter, not harder, was leading to improved Customer experiences in everything that we did.

One of my favorite tools was designed to take a lot of the guesswork out of troubleshooting. Internally the tool was called "Grand Slam" and it worked in every one of the communities that we served. Within seconds, we would be able to do a home health check, knowing almost everything about the Comcast supplied devices in your home. There was even a link that could look at the same information for every home in your neighborhood. This was all done instantly. This changed the game for tech support calls and made identifying issues so much easier. In the past, outages were identified by the number of tickets opened in a geographic area. I still do not know what a ticket really is, but that is a conversation for another day (note, when communicating to Customers, avoid internal jargon like *ticket*). When a large volume of calls came in and piled up, the technical team would declare an outage, but now with the aid of this new tool, the first agent aware of the problem can look at the area and instantly know with certainty if the trouble is at that specific address or somewhere else.

Even with all of this changing, the perceptions were still not changing as rapidly as we had hoped, and we had to drive consistency throughout the organization. How can we make sure that every service experience was consistent in terms of how we helped a Customer? As part of our efforts, leaders from across the company worked to create the Comcast Customer guarantee. It went through many iterations because, as many of you know it is extremely difficult to get everyone on the same page and in agreement, especially if certain actions impact their cost center. But, it was the right thing to do. Here is the Comcast Customer Guarantee:

> **We will give you a 30-day, money-back guarantee on our video, voice, or high-speed services.**
>
> If you're not satisfied with these services and wish to cancel for any reason, you can do so in the first 30 days and get your money back. Simply return all equipment in good working order and we'll refund the monthly recurring fee for your first 30 days of service and any charges you paid for standard installation.
>
> **We will always be on time within your appointment window or we'll credit you $20 or give you a free premium channel for three months.**
>
> As a courtesy, we will call you before we arrive at your home. And if we fail to arrive for a scheduled visit during the appointment window, we will credit you $20 or give you a free premium channel for three months.

We will resolve routine issues in one visit or we'll credit you $20 or give you a free premium channel for three months.

After the first visit to your home, if we do not satisfactorily complete installation or can't resolve a routine issue, we will credit you $20 or give you a free premium channel for three months. Additionally, we won't charge you for a service visit that results from a Comcast equipment or network problem.

We will treat you and your home with courtesy and respect.

Our technicians will display their Comcast identification clearly when they arrive at your home. They will be trained and equipped to complete the job on the first visit. Our Customer Account Executives (CAEs) will be courteous and knowledgeable when you contact us.

We're here for you, 24 hours a day, 7 days a week to answer questions at your convenience.

You can contact us regarding any service-related issue by calling 1–800-COMCAST or in any of the following ways:

> Online, via Ask Comcast
> Live Chat online with a Comcast technician
> Online community forum
> Send us an e-mail and receive a response within 24 hours

We will offer easy-to-understand packages and provide you with a clear bill.

Our packages are designed to be straightforward. A call or visit to our website makes it easy to find a package that's right for you. We aim for the same clarity with our bills. You can view your monthly statement and service details anytime by visiting Comcast Customer Central.

We will continually offer the best and most video choices.

We're working hard to bring more choices to our Customers instantaneously by using the full power of our advanced network and decades of television experience. We will use On Demand to bring you dramatically more content choices, including more movies, more sports, more kids programs, more network TV shows, and more HD than anyone else.

Comcast was moving quickly on the path to changing the Customer experience. As I have mentioned before, the impact of this change does take time to be felt, but as it is an extreme effort being made at even the highest levels of the organization, they are continually working to bring this change to the Customers and have already made positive impacts. At the same time, as they did with Comcast Voices, the company is also marketing these changes in a way that shows the dedication of their employees to the communities and the Customers whom they serve.

CHAPTER

15

Tweet Tweet

Much has been said regarding the Comcast efforts within social media, specifically regarding Twitter. I thought it would be fun to provide a context to the conversation as opposed to the tidbits that you may have read in the past. I have already mentioned our start in social media, which was spurred by Bob Garfield's "Comcast Must Die" website. At this point, efforts to change the organization and the dialogue were hard at work. By the end of 2007, our social outreach was expanding well beyond the initial places where we sought out Customers in need of help. Our efforts through the "Ask Rick" program were providing us with useful information and we were turning many negative experiences into positive ones. We decided that it was time to formalize these programs.

In February 2008, I was asked to take on a new role creating a team to manage the "Ask Rick" program and our digital care efforts, specifically our help forum and social servicing.

We estimated that we would need five people to match the workload that we were currently seeing. We wrote the job descriptions, determined compensation, and began the interview process. Prior to filling new positions, I worked with two employees, Sherri Carson and Mark Casem, to expand our current efforts in social media. We created a daily newsletter to track and report all of the activity that we were seeing regarding the brand on the Internet. I knew from prior experiences that sharing these stories would drive discussion and change within the organization. Here the *Comcast Pulse* newsletter was born. Initially, distribution was limited, going only to a handful of executives, but over the years, recipients grew to include a large number of employees, from all levels within the organization. I started analyzing where discussions were occurring regarding the brand as well as assessing potential tools for listening. Eventually this led to the selection of Radian 6, which I discuss earlier in the book. We were building something brand new, especially in relation to the Customer Service world. Online listening was not new, but usually this was found primarily in PR or marketing, not Customer Service.

Exactly where people were talking online was also changing dramatically. Other than my daughter's website and a handful of websites that I created, I, at the time, was not well versed on the Internet, particularly in sites like LinkedIn, Facebook, or Twitter. After one of our newsletters went out, I received an e-mail from Scott Westerman, a senior leader in New Mexico. He told me about a site called Twitter. I actually remember being overwhelmed looking at it for the first time and I could not possibly guess what the benefits could be. I saw countless short messages on all sorts of topics and at the time there was not even a search capability. I put the site on my watch list, but envisioned no business impact at this point. Within a few weeks, Scott and I began exchanging e-mails about a new website that was bringing search functionality to Twitter. Now I could see some benefits, but the amount of dialogue for any brand was limited.

Meanwhile, we continued our work in identifying places to engage with our Customers. We had a variety of websites that we knew were crucial to keep a close eye on. Places like Broadband Reports, AVS Forum, Tivo Forum, among many others were always worth watching. People were undoubtedly passionate about the Internet and TV! We also started responding to more and more blogs that were talking about Comcast. We would first try to identify the Customer and reach out via phone; if that did not work we would try to locate an e-mail. If neither method proved successful, we would then post a message with our e-mail address. Of course this was opening the door to an entirely new and different communications method to go along with our incoming regular mail, e-mail, fax, phone, chat, and "Ask Rick" program.

As we would reach out to the bloggers we found that reaction was almost always positive. It strikes me as odd, but for some reason, the bloggers we reached out to seemed to think that people did not read their blogs, so when we would call to say we read the blog, they were always thrilled. The reactions often sounded like, "Wow, Comcast read my blog!" Today, only a few years later, I doubt that it would be all that surprising to people. It was definitely a fascinating time for our team! In early April 2008, I was just narrowing down my hiring list to the candidates that seemed to fit best. I concentrated on hiring highly passionate service people, not necessarily those with experience in social media. I felt that I could teach social media, but I could not teach that passion. Looking back years later, this was the right approach. Throughout my tenure at Comcast I treasured and respected my team; I certainly couldn't have done any of this without them. To this day I miss my team's energy and enthusiasm as well as the daily interaction, but I am proud to continue to watch their success in social media.

During the first weekend in April 2008, I was home putting in ceiling fans. Eventually, I decided to climb down from the attic and take a break and stumbled upon a Comcast Google Alert with a post referencing a Twitter conversation that had just started minutes before. I immediately went to Tweetscan, to search for more information. The conversation involved Michael Arrington, founder of TechCrunch, which at the time was one of the most widely read blogs in the world. As I have on other occasions, I searched for his account. Bingo! I picked up the phone and called him immediately. Needless to say, he was surprised. We worked to help him out and the next day he posted a blog titled "Comcast, Twitter, and the Chicken. Trust me I have a Point." When Michael blogs about you, others pick up on it, and the conversation spreads fast across the Internet. Instantly we were outed on Twitter and we had not even posted a tweet yet. As I mentioned, my role had changed a few months earlier to concentrate on social media efforts, so as part of that (and with permission internally) I started to tweet under the @ComcastCares handle. Reaction to Michael's blog post was what you may expect when a media personality gets help. Although Michael Arrington would not consider himself a media personality, at the time he was in fact one of the top online personalities. Commentators' initial reactions were that Comcast only called because it was Michael Arrington. But an amazing thing started to happen. Others we had helped started to chime in on the conversation. Here is an example from someone named Siobhan:

> Actually, they monitor a lot of blogging tools and sites. I have a friend who uses LiveJournal who got an e-mail within about 24 hours of complaining about her Comcast service from a legitimate Customer Service rep, and they sent a tech out to help within a day. So they're doing it whether you're Michael Arrington or the average Joe on the street.

We had instant credibility and support thanks to some of these comments. That was the day when I started tweeting so that we were able to join the conversation and respond. Here is a tweet from @kzimmerman:

> OK . . . now I'm not so skeptical on the Comcast reaction to @TechCrunch. I got a tweet from Comcast less than 10 min. after calling BS on it.

To this day I do not understand how novel an approach people considered this, but the hits kept rolling in. Later that month we started to receive press, including a very nice write-up on the front page of the Sunday edition of the *Philadelphia Inquirer.* You would think our PR staff had pitched the press coverage, but they had not. It was odd and strangely unfamiliar to be part of the spotlight, but at the same time it was helping to reinforce and drive change within the company. It was around this time that we shared the details of our efforts with senior leadership. From the onset they were our biggest fans and best cheerleaders.

I had first met Comcast CEO Brian Roberts on the day my team moved to the new Comcast Center in Philadelphia. We were among the first units to move to the new building. On that day I arrived early to begin settling in. I needed to make sure that the phones were operational and that everything was ready from my team. It was a proud moment for Brian as he was overseeing the company's move into impressive new facilities. He was walking the floor with his family before others arrived. He stepped into my office, and we had a nice bit of small talk about Customer Service and my team. I saw Brian as a family guy and someone much like any of us, who is proud of what his team has been able to accomplish. From our initial conversation to countless others, I saw a man who wanted achievement and triumph for his team, good experiences for his Customers, and success for the business. One of my favorite conversations with Brian occurred a year or two later in a back room of the Cable Show in Washington, DC. Brian and I were having lunch as we were preparing for other activities planned for the day. That weekend he had a couple of phenomenal experiences when interacting with American Express and Amazon. He took the time to share these experiences with me in detail. Next came the big question, "Why couldn't we implement the same technology that these firms were using?" Of course we could, but it would take time and effort to create and implement other underlying programming changes in order to make it effective. The technology being used by American Express and Amazon provided clear information to the Customer for specific wait times and the option to choose a callback. It was a fun and energizing conversation. Moreover, seeing such a senior leader engaged in this type of conversation was motivating. Customer Service is not a difficult field; you just need to think like a Customer and he was doing just that. We did eventually get the technology implemented.

Over the years, I have occasionally seen Brian painted in a very negative light and this saddens me. Most notably there is an article from *Wired Magazine* referring to him as the "Dark Lord of Broadband." The article mainly focuses on some issues at Comcast regarding network management that were highlighted in May 2007. I joined Comcast a few months later, so I do not have intimate knowledge of how the organization was at that time. CEOs are often painted with a brush based on the actions of the company, without fully interpreting other aspects of how decisions were made. I am sure that some of the decisions high-lighted in the article were made by others, but as it often happens, he seemed to be the one to take the fall. The Dark Lord article itself probably played well to the audience of *Wired Magazine*, so prior to its release I should have suspected a dark undertone. The end of the article had some nice words to say about the work of my team and me, which of course I appreciated, but I have to acknowledge that our work could not have been done without Brian's support and I will be forever grateful for it. Knowing that he was on our side made it much easier to achieve everything we did. The article itself was clearly written in a *Star Wars*-esque style with Brian portrayed as Darth Vader. My wife thinks that it may have (intentionally or unintentionally) portrayed me as Luke Skywalker in the story, and since the article appeared, my wife and I have affectionately referred to Brian as "my dad"! I never told him about that, but I guess he may find out now.

Now let me get back to Twitter. As all of this was going on, Twitter search was still a new functionality but it was proving to be very useful and changing the landscape of social media. Prior to Twitter, Customer conversations in most social spaces took place after you had messed something up, but with Twitter, because of the way it was being utilized, it could be used as an early warning system. Often information was available on Twitter before a Customer even called in. Today Twitter asks the question "What's Happening?" Back then it was "What are you Doing?" And people would tell you exactly that: "I am calling Comcast right now." Using Twitter search, we could often tell why people were calling before they had even picked up the phone. We then had the opportunity to respond with offers of assistance and take care of them right there.

For the first six months or so, I was the only member of my team on Twitter. Due to the publicity that we were receiving in conjunction with the volumes, my hiring count went from five to seven representatives. Later in 2008, we increased the team to ten, where it would stay over the next few years. Continued publicity resulted in additional blog posts and I was still trying to figure out how to operate Twitter. I worried that a wrong move could be detrimental to our efforts. In the early days, I was tweeting as @ComcastCares in the early morning, all day, night, late night, and virtually whenever I could. This meant that I was usually working around the clock, seven days a week. People were critiquing almost everything that I did. Most likely at that time, you could count the number of businesses on Twitter on one hand. We were all just trying to figure out the right way to do things. One blog post talked about my use of the word *perception*. I responded via Twitter with something like, "I am sorry that we created that perception for you." The blogger was wondering who speaks that way! Of course, I did and I still do, but every time I read something, I try to learn from it. What I took from that post was that I was being too proper and needed to loosen up, so that is exactly what I did. We learned a lot through those early days.

A major aha moment for me, and one that I think other brands could benefit from, came in July 2008. I was on Twitter for four months under the @ComcastCares handle, developing plans to have other members of my team participate on the handle, but I was still working out how to operate it. On July 25 I tweeted that I would not be available the next day. I did not get into why, but I will tell you now that we were having a birthday party for our daughter who turned two on the 25th. The next day also had a different significance in that it was the anniversary of our daughter Gia's death. As I mentioned earlier, we had a website that we utilized to communicate with family and friends during Gia's life, and it remains out there. Anyway, I was sitting with some friends having a few drinks when I looked on my computer through the typical Twitter search and I noticed an amazing thing: Others were responding to those in need of Comcast help or support. Some of the tweets said "Let's let @ComcastCares have his day, can I help you?" Others shared advice that they were given to correct similar trouble. Amazingly, these tweets went on all day long. They were not from other employees, but from actual Customers. Would you help Customers of your cable provider that you didn't even know? Those who were helping on Twitter were not doing it for Comcast; instead they were doing it for me. Social media is an incredibly personal space built with human connections. Companies often miss this fact and try to concentrate on the message instead of the human nature of their own employees.

This story had a profound impact on the way I look at social media for business, but also in the way that Comcast was going about our servicing strategy. Immediately, I changed my avatar to my picture. I also listed my family website and later my blog, along with the typical links to business.

New team members were provided with their own Twitter handles. They were able to choose their avatar and they were encouraged to be themselves. One of the team members did not want to share her picture, so instead she chose a butterfly. Another team member chose a picture in which she is holding her beautiful baby. One day while going through her normal search, she came across someone who was a little upset. She offered to help this Customer via Twitter. The Customer tweeted back to say that since she had that particular avatar, he would not yell at her. In essence, the avatar humanized the employee in the eyes of the Customer. This human touch is what has been missing from most businesses' social media efforts. Service, whether on the phones or via Twitter, is still all about this human interaction. In this story, he did not see her as Comcast, but instead as the person she really is.

And so, Twitter became a key aspect to our early warning system. People throughout the organization were watching Twitter to build understanding, gain insights, and improve the Customer or employee experience. You could find almost anything that you could ever want or imagine just by searching. We gained incredible amounts of insight and feedback, usually much faster than possible via any other channel.

The speed of information via Twitter was becoming more and more obvious to us. One of the better examples of this came during an NHL playoff game between the Pittsburgh Penguins and the Philadelphia Flyers. Fox Sports Net went off the air.

We saw a rash of tweets the moment this happened, even before any calls came in. Comcast-Spectacor, the owner of the Flyers, is partially owned by Comcast. Some of the tweets were amusing; accusing us of taking the game off the air because we were losing. Obviously this is not true! Using Twitter search, we were able to identify the cause as a lightning strike in Atlanta where the feed generates. We found that it was also impacting other channels throughout the country. We were able to quickly relay this information to our call center, update the message for those calling in, and alert the engineers to the actual cause. All this was done in a matter of minutes. You can then measure the calls that come in, receive the message, and then hang up. Each one is a saved cost to the business, yet you are able to provide the caller with a good experience with detailed information.

CHAPTER

16

Driving Change in an Organization

It was not all fun or constant success at Comcast. There were many bumps in the long, winding road, which is to be expected whenever change is happening in an organization. The important thing is to understand where Customers are coming from and try to provide them the context they need in return. Social media is live and open for the world to see, and sometimes your company needs to be open as well. This is against the grain of how businesses have traditionally worked, as many companies prefer a controlled message approach. The downside to that is that others are already having the conversation out there without the company.

Product leaders sometimes get upset over commentary from Customers or service representatives, whether it is during calls or broadcast via social media. This is because as leaders, we tend to be passionate about our product, and we would never want to see negative commentary from anyone. However, sometimes negative feedback is imperative to bring about change. If something is not working, it makes sense to alert someone that it is not working and ask when he or she can expect it to be working again. Customers do not like canned responses, as they would like to know that you are listening to them and that you understand their needs.

The other challenge is that in social media or during a Customer call, you do not always have time to wait for businesses to make a decision. Imagine if you called a company with a complaint and the representative said nothing regarding the issue. Or how would you feel if the representative responded with, "I am waiting to hear what I can say!" Would it add to the trust you have for the company or the service team? Of course not.

So how do you get leaders to take a different view and increase their willingness to open up? Actually, that is the easy part. If you are taking Customer Service calls, share the actual calls with them. Review the specifics together. Maybe leaders could join your service team during the next issue. In social media, share the commentary that is being made. Ask for help in how you might respond. Beyond all this, share the Customer feedback regarding how the interactions go. Customers crave openness and knowing that someone is on their side; business leaders want to see Customers having a good experience with your company. As time goes on, leaders will realize the benefits of the openness and as they embrace it they will come to you asking for the company to do it more frequently. The first step is not being afraid to do it.

It is important that through all of this you have senior leader support. At Comcast our leadership was dedicated to what we were striving to do and, even if they did not fully understand, you knew they had your back, even when mistakes were made.

I did the same for my team members in everything that they did. As a result, they were empowered and encouraged to create new and even better experiences for our Customers. I wanted to constantly try new things, even knowing that some might not work as intended. But at least I could say that we tried. Do you have your employees' backs? Too often, especially in larger process driven organizations, we send the opposite message.

The Customer Guarantee, similar to a corporate mission and vision, has a way of getting everyone in an organization on the same playing field. Once on that field, you are on a path toward improvement, but change may take years to reach the level you are pursuing. How do you accelerate this change? How do you drive change quickly in an organization that is not centralized in approach and provides a certain level of autonomy?

Advanta showed me how to do this through the power of Customer stories. Throughout all of the data that leaders are bombarded with daily, it is often hard to see the direct impact on the Customer. At Comcast, we interacted with Customers over 300 million times a year through service, tech support, or technician visits. That is a lot of interactions and a lot of procedures to review. You can use statistics to drive that, but you would miss a lot. Even if 99 percent of those interactions were perfect, it would still leave three million that needed improvement. Although one percent does not sound bad, three million poor Customer interactions sounds awful. We also know that brand reputation is often driven by Customer experiences. This was always the case with traditional media, which is one of the reasons why companies often handled reporters with kid gloves, but, in the social world, anyone and everyone can now be that reporter. The key is getting it right!

We accelerated change at Comcast through our daily newsletter. We typically did not concentrate on data, but on the Customer stories that we came across. When possible, we would even highlight the area in which the Customer resided. The newsletter went to many executives and gave them a true look at the brand perception. We would first highlight some high level information, such as popular websites talking about the brand. We then had a section that changed daily, such as YouTube Fridays where we highlighted videos from the week. One day each week we would share pictures found on Twitter, and often they would be photos of lines at various offices. Pictures would generate a lot of discussion from the executives on the distribution. The next sections highlighted blog discussion and forums. We also included news to present a complete daily picture of our brand in action.

Although the newsletter highlighted stories, we focused on the human element whenever possible. One example was a blogger named Grannie Annie. She lived in an area that was being taken over by Comcast from another cable provider, and she was having some difficulty with the process. Simply supplying data would have shown others with the same trouble, but sharing the story of Grannie Annie puts a face to the issue and demands your attention. Simply stating that X number of Customers has been impacted does not grab attention.

You can even have a little fun with the information you share! In 2008, Jeff Jarvis wrote an article for Bloomberg's *BusinessWeek* called "Love the Customers Who Hate You." These are still Customers that are incredibly passionate about your brand because the opposite of love is really apathy, not hate. Anyway, in the article Jeff educated people about understanding their brand and searching their brand name with the word *sucks* after it. Let's take this a step further. When you do a search on Google, it provides a quantity of results. You can then do this for other brands, or really anything, and compare the data. It can be fascinating to look at your brand versus others in your industry. You can then map to the quantity of results over time as long as you are consistent in the approach. I referred to it as the "Google 'Sucks'

Index." People have a lot of fun seeing data that they can access simply by searching Google. They also enjoyed seeing other brands they were familiar with. Finding perspective that works with your audience can drive change.

I am a passionate Customer advocate in everything I do, but there are times when lack of knowledge can help lead direction. While at Comcast my lack of cable experience forced me to ask questions constantly. Why did we do certain things? Why were certain procedures in place? Most often I already knew the answers but I was guiding the direction of the conversation and bringing people to my thoughts. Often when you look at procedures, what made sense at one point, no longer does. This sometimes can be better seen by someone not as close to the procedure.

Another way to lead change is surrounding yourself with leaders who are striving to do the same. Change and energy are contagious! Rick Germano is an impressive leader and a great asset to Comcast because of the respect that others have for him in addition to his deep understanding of the organization. Company-wide meetings of the service team leaders took place frequently. Sometimes gaining agreement is not easy, especially without the authority over groups that a centralized team may have. But Rick did this often with finesse. For example, we had been trying to get every unit to use the Grand Slam tool that I discussed earlier. There are always a million reasons not to do something, and we were hearing it all. After Rick had every-one present his or her views, he turned to me and said, "Frank, how do you and your team use the tool?" In response, I walked everyone through the process that my team was using. It was not the usual operating procedures that were used prior to our having the tool, but the process we used made complete sense to us and the Customers we were serving. The tool allowed us to provide more definitive information to the Customer regarding their current situation, such as whether a tech was needed at their location or we needed to have work done in the area. By looking at this separately from the traditional approach, our commentary helped others see the benefits and accept and start to build the new process that would best serve our Customers. Teamwork with Rick was key to driving something that we were both interested in seeing happen. Partner with others in your organization to create buy in and drive change.

Our efforts at Comcast were also working to change and improve the cable industry as a whole. Following Comcast's lead, other providers are working hard to change the experience that they create for their Customers. One of the best ways to lead is by example. To the public eye, what my team was doing was showing that there could be a different approach to serving cable Customers. When I was in call center management, I was never afraid to take a call from a Customer and show others how it can be done right. I have used this mentality for years to inspire my team and create a winning environment. Do you get in the trenches and lead by example?

Ultimately, the key is building as much understanding as you can, and when you do not know, ask questions. Asking why can be a powerful way to generate change. Questions also have the unique ability to drive people to the same conclusions that you already have in your mind. People do not realize the power that they hold, and I have found that employees at all levels of the organization can drive change. It's time for each of us to start asking the right questions!

CHAPTER

17

Social Customer Service Is a Failure

While much work was being done at Comcast in the public view, an even greater amount of work was being done internally and away from the spotlight. Social media in business, in my view, has often been a failure for a multitude of reasons. More importantly, social media Customer Service, which some have credited me with starting, is probably a larger failure. Although I think that a few companies, including Comcast, continue to do the right things, others are not performing to the level that they should, and in many ways, may be hurting their brand in the process.

Our efforts at Comcast were centered on improving service for our Customers. In watching many other organizations, I am not sure that they have that same concentration. Most organizations still strive to control the message so they concentrate any social media service efforts within PR or marketing. Often their main reason for even offering to help someone in social media is to put an end to negative conversation. In doing so, they often may make exceptions or strive to treat that particular Customer differently from the way they would through other channels. All Customers should be treated fairly and consistently. By making exceptions for those who are speaking out, it appears that their only goal is striving to shut up their Customer and not necessarily on fixing the underlying issues. Ultimately, the message that this type of company is unknowingly and unintentionally sending is that the best way to get what you want is to complain publicly. This will not bring about a long-term win in social media!

Companies are now advertising their social servicing through many channels, as they believe that Customers want this type of service. The reality is that Customers just want a really good experience in the channel that they choose, which is often not in public spaces. If a Customer has a bad experience, then they often resort to blasting the company within social media. You can review any of the service-oriented blowups that companies have had, and all had other interactions first. As an example, Kevin Smith had an issue with Southwest Airlines that lit up Twitter in 2010. In that incident, according to Southwest, Mr. Smith had bought two tickets for a flight, but decided to go standby for an earlier flight. They then ticketed him and let him board. After he had dealt with ticketing agents and boarding personnel, he was allowed to have the seat, but after he was seated, Southwest decided to eject him due to their policy of requiring multiple tickets for people of size. Note that he did have two tickets prior to going standby. So during this scenario, Mr. Smith dealt with a variety of members of the Southwest team through a variety of channels prior to venting his frustrations on Twitter. In another well-known incident involving United Airlines, Dave Carroll had a number of interactions with the company regarding his broken guitar. Eventually he gave up on interacting directly with the company and took the incident to YouTube in the form of a song. More than eleven million people have now viewed the video.

The first aspect of social service is recognizing that the Customer does have control over your brand and that your service, no matter how hard you try, may not always live up to your organization's expectations or the expectations of the Customer. The next aspect is working to correct this as much as possible. We discuss more about what is really broken in the coming chapters, so you will be able to improve your service center.

Companies or their salespeople may tell you that social service is cheaper than other communications channels. That argument is typically false. First, how often does someone tweet you for service? What is the approval process for a tweet? What is the brand cost for the negative conversation even if the right things happen in the end?

One of the reasons that I chose Citi was because of their CMO's dedication to creating the right experiences for Customers through all methods of communications. The attitude of this CMO is admirable and should be something that leaders of all companies should be striving for. How do we make it right for our Customer? Doing things right will encourage Customers to spread a positive message for the brand and build it up instead of tearing it down in social media.

We mentioned listening earlier; it is one of the key reasons I think that social servicing is failing. Listening has not become a core process throughout the organization; it is usually centralized in PR waiting for that next crisis to hit. Bring listening to the forefront of your organization. It will provide insight to product designers, leaders, and the entire service organization. Now broaden the listening to include other key topics such as competitors or interest groups. The information can help the entire organization.

I am also not sure why listening is geared specifically toward social media, when Customers are talking to you every day through a variety of channels. There are many tools that can help add data of all types, including the words spoken in calls, e-mails, or chat sessions. Now is the time to look at everything that you do and work toward building a business that people will want to talk about.

18

An Inside Look at a Call Center

Let's take a visit to a call center. Some of you may work in one, others may have drifted through, but some may never have had the opportunity to experience daily life in one, although we have certainly all called one! Over the years, I have had the privilege of working in many different call centers and visiting even more. Please note that the following scenarios outlined are not specific to any call center that I have worked in or have done business with, and you will want to thoroughly investigate the ins and outs of life in your call center after reading this. It is so very important to know exactly what is going on in your call center because the impact on the Customer is enormous. This is often how your Customer sees you or hears your message. Please try to wear all hats when reading the following, especially the Customer's hat. If your business does not have a call center, you can still think of this through the mind of your frontline employees and the Customers you serve.

Imagine that today is your first day on the job as a new Customer Service representative. You walk in and see balloons and what appears to be a happy place. You check in with HR and are brought into a classroom. As you were walking to the classroom, you thought about how thrilled you were that you found a job where you can help people. At the front of the training room stands a cheery trainer excited to have you and the rest of the new recruits onboard. Training will be anywhere from a few days to a few weeks depending on the type of call center it is. During the training they teach you the basic technical aspects to the job: usually the system that you will utilize and the knowledge base to obtain information to answer Customer questions. Often you will not be taught exactly what to say, but you will be referred to the talking points in the knowledge base. The systems can be confusing because many companies use multiple programs. This adds to the complications of the new job because you will be expected to know how to use each one.

Nevertheless, training is always a happy time, even when you get to go out on the floor to listen to calls. They will probably sit you with the best representatives at the company. These individuals are usually very nice and they always follow the rules to the letter, at least in the eyes of their manager. During the training process, trainees split time from the classroom to on-the-job training and listening to calls. As time goes on, agents start to share the reality of working in a call center. The first thing they do is start to go over pain points that Customers have and what, if anything, can be done to counteract this. Sometimes you will learn shortcuts and workarounds that are not demonstrated during training. Finally, the conversation shifts to the different managers and their styles.

Toward the end of training, a manager comes in to go over the rules. Much time is spent on attendance and behavior policies, emphasizing how you will be fired if you do not abide by them. You are now starting to wonder if some of the representatives are thinking that the balloons decorating the call center may be more appropriate in a day care center. The manager also spends time going over how your performance will be measured and what this means to you. Typical call center metrics will be average handle time, or how long you have spent with each Customer, compliance to scripts or quality, adherence to your schedule, attendance, and finally sales. Often the expectation is that you will sell on every call, whether it is appropriate or not. You can easily spot these call centers when you are a Customer calling with a problem; before the representative addresses the reason for your call they'll try to sell you something. This is simply the agent trying to meet the quality goals, and this is part of the checklist.

You now start to take live calls, usually with a buddy right next to you. This is when you will learn all sorts of things that weren't covered in the training class. Calls come in and they let you go listening half-heartedly because they are just excited to be off the phone for a little while. The cube that you are sitting in is fairly close to the person next to you and the noise level is high due to all the talking. During this nesting period, all is well but it does not last long. Suddenly you hear beeps across the floor and red digital signs are blinking. You see the manager walking around yelling at everyone to get on the phones. Your buddy jumps up and says that you are on your own, as she makes her way back to her desk to take calls. The next call comes through and now you are flustered with no help. You are hitting the keyboard going through each of the systems, trying to find the right answer, but with no luck. The Customer is getting irritated at the lack of help and is sniping in your ear. You try to ask those around you, but they are busy with their own calls. Finally you get up to ask the supervisor, who snaps back that the answer is in the knowledge base. Frustrated, you go back to look again. Finally, the Customer hangs up without the right answer and another call comes through even before you are ready to start again. Now even more flustered, you struggle with the next call and they wish to escalate as the caller hears the uncertainty in your voice. You go searching the floor for your supervisor and he is nowhere to be found.

Finally, another representative whom you sat with during training offers to take the call for you. Now you have some relief. After the call has been completed, you need to go to the restroom. So you place your phone in break mode to go. When you return, your supervisor is at your desk asking where you have been. He explains that you are not scheduled for break until later in the morning and asks why you only took a handful of calls.

Certainly this has not been a good day and definitely not a great start compared to the high hopes that you had for this new job. As you get back on the phones, you get a call from a Customer whom you want to help. You understand precisely what she needs, but the call will take a while. You think, I can't have another long call, but there is no choice. Then the Customer, who greatly appreciates how well you are listening and the understanding that you seem to have, says that she has to run but wants to call back and speak directly to you. Unfortunately, policy and the phone system that the company uses do not allow you to give the Customer your extension. During training you were told to simply tell the Customer, "Everyone is able to help you just as well as I can. Just simply call back at a time that is convenient for you and they will care for you." With this the Customer, who is now yelling, says that she has called six times and you were the first one to understand. They then hang the phone up out of frustration.

Interestingly, many call centers are designed not to have personal phone extensions. This was based on the business decision that Customers might call the same person back frequently or they might call and leave a message, but the agent might not follow up or have that extension anymore, in effect causing a worse Customer experience. There can also be a concern that the agents will take personal calls.

The next call comes through and it is regarding a policy that Customers do not like. You heard all about this during training and reviewed many calls on the topic. The answer is always the same, so you provide it. You have yet to hear a call where the Customer was thankful for the answer. You read the answer directly from the script that references this as instructed and the Customer yells in the same manner as the last caller. The company requires you to end every call the same way and ask, "Is there anything else that I can do to help you today?" In response, the Customer yells back, "You have not helped me yet, so why start now?" The phone slams down. After that call you are late for break, so you go. Upon return the supervisor is right there at your workstation again stating that you are late coming back from break. You then explain that the call lasted after the start of your break so you went as soon as you could.

Once again you are back to the phones. As the calls come in you notice that your system is running slower and slower. You help the Customers as best you can, but it is taking minutes for an account to even come up on the screen. At one point you apologize to the Customer for how slow the system is. You eventually help them out, but when you have finished, you look up and the supervisor is back at your desk. He is upset because he was listening to the call, heard internal jargon regarding the systems, and is really upset that you told the Customer how slow the system is. You ask what else could have been said during the lull while waiting for it to come up. He responds, "Anything but that" as he walks back to his desk.

As time goes on, you start to get a little more comfortable but realize there is not all that much that you can change. You stick to the procedures outlined and you do your job. You watch the clock. Eventually the mirror that they gave you during training to encourage you to smile during calls breaks but you leave it hanging on the wall. Broken tchotchkes are not an uncommon site in a call center.

Often, a career for a Customer Service agent is not as pleasant as it should be and coworkers who often want to escape the Customer surround you. At many companies, service is at a location with other business units, and you will find that employees in the other areas look down on the agents and the job as something that is clearly beneath them. This sends a message to those serving your Customers about the focus of the company. Although there are excellent supervisors and managers out there, many are burnt out and many others worked their way up in similar conditions so they are not that interested in changing them.

Customer Service is often an entry-level position. Ongoing training is usually not available to advance the career of the Customer Service representative; it is usually just available for business reasons such as new products or mandatory compliance or systems training. The center is managed to the expected call volume with limited or no excess. Due to budget, resources, training, and other reasons, off phone time is usually not available. The agents are hungry for pay, so they will often work all the overtime available without complaint.

Supervisors and managers often prefer to hire people who do not question policies, as these individuals are the easiest to manage. Turnover rates are typically high in call centers because the better performers have an easy time finding new jobs, often at other companies, while mediocre or poor performers are managed out. It is not often that performance is improved, even with coaching. Coaching is typically along the lines of "You need to do x" but little help to actually achieving it is offered.

Policies are often extremely rigid, and the scripts reflect that. People in other business areas often drive the policies, and areas like marketing usually write the scripts. The trouble with this way of doing things is that employees in other business areas do not always understand the impact of the policies and how they affect both the Customer and the service agent. With scripts, the problem is that the Customer does not have the other side of the script. Customers have many communication styles and don't always know exactly what to ask. It would be easier and more effective to better train the employees and provide insights into the reasoning behind policies. Armed with this knowledge, Customer Service representatives could question or provide feedback to the right people internally when a policy is getting in the way unintentionally. Empowerment is not giving away the store; it is providing people with the connections that they need to achieve the right business results. Empowerment will result in employee and Customer satisfaction.

Agents often do not have one-on-ones with their manager unless it is part of a disciplinary path. The supervisors are often overworked and managing teams of 20–25 or more people. Of course, the supervisors are also handling escalated calls and helping team members throughout the day. Ultimately, this leaves little time for supervisors to focus on employee development.

Systems are also not designed to deal with things outside the norm, such as an error made by an employee. This naturally causes great irritation to Customers. Have you ever called a place with what you knew was a complicated situation? The agent's initial response is often to state that that simply can't happen. This is certainly not what the Customer wants to hear! Recently my wife ordered clocks featuring personalized maps of actual addresses from *National Geographic* to send as gifts. Four out of five clocks were perfect, but one was blatantly wrong. Although clock number five was labeled properly, the map itself was for two towns over. (Please note that we did submit the correct address with the order!) The address simply could not be found on this clock! Within the package there was a slip stating that even though this map may look different from the way our town is designed today, it is accurate, because the maps used to make the clock were older. I called about this and the agent took the same position outlined on the package slip. I explained that I had grown up in the area and the map was totally inaccurate; in fact, it was off by about five miles. Finally we realized the issue and eventually their representative was able to quickly send out a corrected clock. It turns out that the program used to design the clocks uses Google Maps to map the area and design the clock. For this particular address, for whatever reason, Google changed it to a different address two towns over.

Back to our call center! You would think that call centers are naturally focused on reducing the overall volume but usually they are focused more on the here and now. As high call volumes come in, managers shift to managing staff to get through quantity over quality, and quality suffers when they are focusing on quantity. Unfortunately, this usually leads to repeat calls, which end up being more costly than spending the time and getting it right at the initial conversation. Many call centers have adopted and learned to live with an "is what it is" mentality, which means they do not strive to drive change throughout the organization, but rather deal with the issues as they are.

The best call center agents are often highly passionate for the Customer but are frustrated by policies that impact their ability to help. Over time, they become resourceful and find ways to work through them. Unfortunately, they are also in the minority. To many agents working in a call center, it is just a job and a paycheck.

The CBS show, *Undercover Boss*, features the world of the call center in a number of episodes. Before you complain that the show is highly choreographed, focus on the lesson. Although it can come across as contrived, it is still interesting to see how they present some of their Customer interactions and the front lines of the business. One of my favorite episodes shows a CEO flustered by the incoming calls.

One of the challenges that CEOs and other leaders face is gaining direct insight into what these interactions are like. Customer Service employees, like most other people, want to show themselves in the most positive light possible. It is important for a leader to make it safe to demonstrate the real world in which they live. Of course this should be done throughout the organization whenever possible, but it is imperative in the Customer Service world since they are the ones with the most power over your brand and continued sales.

You may want to think about taking your own Undercover Boss challenge. No, you do not have to go on the show. You don't even have to give away a lot of money. (Of course, some of your frontline employees might like the rewards and perks!) Go where the employees are and just chat. Chances are, they would be happy to tell you all about life in the call center. Meet them in their space, which might be in the break room, outside, or wherever they eat lunch. First, listen to the conversations that are already happening to get a feel for what is going on. You will get a good idea of how morale is in your call center. Once you are more comfortable, talk to individuals and groups with a friendly and understanding demeanor. As you build trust with them they will provide you with more and more information.

If you have an opportunity to sit side by side with an agent while listening to calls, realize that it is highly likely that you are sitting with one of the best representatives. Management may have also coached those around the representative whom you are sitting with to be on her best behavior. Still, try to find ways to make connections. This will break down the barriers that the coaching caused, and then information will flow more rapidly. Talk to them about their frustrations. You will find it is usually not their managers (although it can be sometimes); it is usually the policies that make their job difficult. Phone representatives often start to think that no one in the organization cares about the Customer. You have the ability to change that with a few words of inspiration!

If you work in a larger company, you might want to consider Googling your brand with the words *call center* and *employee*. You might find some interesting tales that make up your brand to anyone who comes across these stories. I searched the web for one brand and came across thousands of examples. How would you like to see comments like the following?

- "Getting bitched at all day does not do much for your company morale and makes you less likely to want to help anyone. Follow that up with incentive plans based on the number of calls per day you handle, and BOOM . . . the anti-CSR is born."

- "I work in the [REDACTED] call center. For the most part, the job is good, and the benefits are fabulous. However, management and human resources do the best they can to come up with ways to fire people. They have an attendance policy that keeps track of your BATHROOM visits. If you are away from your desk for more than eight minutes, you are assessed five points and fifteen minutes of UNPAID time. There is entirely too much pressure from the supervisors to sell things we haven't even been trained on. You only get quota relief if you go on vacation for five consecutive days . . . not if you are in training for three days."

- "This company stinks!!!! It was the worst place I have ever worked. I was a manager and I hated almost every minute of it there. They change policies on a daily basis. You never know who to call. If you do have a problem and have to call someone expect to be on the phone (on hold) forever. There's not enough money to get me back there EVER!!"

- "They would micromanage us like children."

Today your brand message is created by many, especially as it now includes the employee experience. This particular employer outsourced some of their call center work; yet often the brand received the same blame that the actual employer received. They have since been working to change the brand perception. One of the first steps that they took was to correct some of this mistreatment, but the damage was already done. It is out there for the world to see whenever someone thinks to search for it. I imagine that it still has impact on those considering a career with this company. Would you want to be an employee for this company? How about a Customer? I am sure many of you are!

19

The Basic Tenets of Service

The service industry has been going through an identity crisis for years, and it is important to recognize this and understand the reasons why. Overall, service is usually one of the highest costs to any business big or small. This has led to a common discussion of service being the "cost center." In an effort to change this internal perception, well-intentioned leaders tried to convert the call center into the "sales center." We have all had this backfire when we have called for help and the person on the phone could only focus on the wrong thing. As time moves forward, especially with the Customer having a much larger control over your brand, it is imperative that we begin to see service as the "relationship hub."

On rare occasions, especially if your organization has properly focused efforts on reducing calls, you have an opportunity to interact with your Customer in a memorable way. Tony Hsieh from Zappos often tells the story of hanging out with some vendors when someone in the group wanted pizza. Tony told them to call Zappos. Would you think to call a shoe retailer for pizza? Anyway, as you can guess, they called Zappos and the representative helped them find pizza places in their area that delivered to the hotel. I do not tell this story expecting that your service organization will start becoming the concierge for all kinds of services and products, but the story is a great example of how Zappos is willing to be a little different in their quest to build relationships with their Customers. Imagine if this happened to you, would you be wowed?

The challenge to service is defining what it means within your organization and then living it at all levels. Most organizations try to say that they are all about the Customer but in reality they are more for the shareholders and profit than anything else. Clearly there is nothing wrong with being focused on shareholders and profits. The key is being true to who you are. Zappos lives their values in everything they do.

There are numerous books out there that will teach you all kinds of fancy catch phrases or themes to build the right service experience. I will not try to come up with some really cool acronym. The themes that really win are some of the basics:

- Treat people the way you would want to be treated.
- Listen to your Customer.
- Empower your employees.
- Value your Customer's time.

Simply put, these bulleted items say, "Appreciate your Customer and your employees!"

Courtesy is easy, and it is something that we all learned from our parents and teachers from the beginning; yet, it seems in this ever busy world, we forget the importance of it as we get older. Many calls that I have heard come across sounding like no one cares, and that is deplorable. We can unknowingly send out these messages when our Customer contacts us through a call center. They are first trapped in the IVR making it nearly impossible to escape! As you know, most IVRs appear to be circuitous. Getting a live person on the phone can sometimes be difficult! As an example, many organizations force you to listen to account information through the automated system prior to even providing the opportunity to speak to someone. Does that show courtesy?

Listening is an overused term nowadays, yet we are still not good at listening whether it is social media, Customer Service, or within our own company. We are constantly bombarding our Customers with surveys, yet often not using what they say. (Not using their feedback sends a message to them whether you realize it or not.) Do not be afraid to show ways in which you are listening in your advertising or other interactions. This does not mean starting a marketing campaign saying that you listen to Customers. That, too, is often overdone, and people do not always believe these types of marketing messages, as they are shallow and lack substance. The real marketing is when your own Customers will come out and say, "Wow, XYZ Company is listening!" This happens when they feel that you understand their issues and are doing something about them. Of course, it can also happen when you exceed their expectations or wow them. Listening effectively can result in huge marketing wins.

One day, I decided to share feedback with an organization. My feedback was very detailed regarding my experience and outlined why I would not be making a major purchase with them in the future. I decided not to share the name of the brand but understand that it is one that most readers of this book deal with somewhat frequently. After spending the time writing out my thoughts, I received the following response:

Frank,

Thank you for contacting us. I'm so sorry about your experience. We are making many improvements under our leader [REDACTED CEO Name]. I apologize that you did not see those improvements during your attempt to order. Thank you for taking the time to share your feedback. It is important for our continued growth.

Please let us know if there's anything that we can do to assist you in the future.

Thanks,

Stephanie

My written response to the organization was that I did not think they truly cared and that their e-mail went into the typical black hole. How often are we sending responses that create this feeling? I am sure that you have numerous examples when you felt that companies were not listening to you. Do you ever send that message to your Customers?

Empowerment of your employees is probably the least enabled method today yet has the power to drive the greatest Customer satisfaction. Empowerment does not mean "giving away the store," as some strongly believe. *Empowerment* should mean that your frontline employees have the ability to get the right people involved to review experiences and ensure that the right decisions are made. If they feel a policy is impacting a Customer, they should be able to escalate the concern, with change happening fast. As a Customer, which would you rather hear?

- No!
- Sorry, there is nothing that I can do.
- They do not allow us to do that.
- Thank you for the feedback. I am not able to change this right now, but I can see exactly where you are coming from.

Let me get the right team members involved and we will see what options we can come up with. I will follow up with you.

Now obviously the ideal scenario is that the agent is able to rectify the situation during the call, but if this is not possible, the response becomes more difficult. Often it is, "I am sorry we are not able to do that and I will share the feedback." You have probably heard employees respond with something like, "They do not let us." As a Customer, you probably wonder who "they" is. Well, it is the management of the company that you are calling. Although it is very possible that the employee is referring to their immediate supervisor, it is ultimately the business leader whom they are speaking of. I cringe each and every time that I hear this, but often it is just a policy that the agent may not agree with or understand. It is human nature to shift the blame to someone else.

Time is valuable to all of us but the service world often focuses on the wrong time. We track handle time from a budget and business perspective, but if we were to focus on the Customer's time, it would have more impact and can lead to the same results. Customers do not usually want to talk to their service provider. They are doing so because they have a need that is not being filled and thus must contact the service provider. They want their problem fixed. Wait times are just one way that we add to their frustration. Do you like to shop at places with long lines or short lines? I may be more willing to stand in line at a discount store, but if I am paying a premium, probably not. Where I get the most frustrated is when I am standing in line and I see other employees watching the lines, but not doing anything to reduce them. I like to see managers jump in and help out to care for their Customers.

When I was sixteen years old, I worked at a regional discount chain called Clover. If you are old enough and lived in the

Philadelphia area I am sure that you remember the chain and probably still miss it. While I was there I received a lot of lessons on servicing Customers, both good and bad, and I still reference those lessons in everything that I do. One of these lessons taught me how to value the Customer's time over company policy or procedure. I worked part-time stocking shelves and working with the store managers on renovations. On a particularly busy weekend, they had everyone possible at the registers. One of the store managers turned to me and asked how comfortable I would be using the register. I was not trained at the time, so it would have been a blatant violation of the policy for me to use one. The manager's point was that sales and the Customers were more important than any policy and she fully trusted me to do the right thing. A few days later, I was walking into the manager's office to check in when I overheard a conversation that she was having with the HR team regarding the decision. Obviously they were not thrilled that she was not following the rules. She focused the conversation back to the Customers and explained that Customers were her priority. It is always hard to come back from that argument. She then asked specific questions about sales during the period and my specific performance on the register.

All of these points, when put together, underscore the importance of showing appreciation for the Customer and the employee. Empowerment demonstrates trust in your employee. Focusing on the Customer's needs creates a more favorable experience and an employee who enjoys their job will present the right image for your company. The trouble that we have had in recent years is that we have tried to make everything about process and metrics. By taking the human element out of things, we have taken away the human emotion, making it difficult to succeed in a world driven by our human Customers. Customers share information with their friends based on emotion. Your employees do the same when they are excited by what they do.

As Seth Godin pointed out in *Linchpin*, today's business world is often run as if it were the Industrial Age, and employees are part of that assembly line no matter what their role is. In my opinion, the Customer Service world, in recent years, has become the epitome of this view. At one time, Customer Service was about providing great experiences. But as time went on and companies got larger, we tried to make it more and more process driven, resulting in the world we live in today. It is not hard to break from that model, but it does require us to think about how we can escape the past and move on. In some ways, it requires us to start to think like a small business owner again, one who has a passion for what he is doing and is extremely close to the Customer. We need to bring the Customer Service world to be key in your organization. This will get Customers to talk!

CHAPTER

20

Is Service One of Your Values?

The Customer Service world has changed dramatically over the past fifty years. What started as hard-lined phones with handsets and runners with paper has changed to websites, IVR, computer desktops, wireless headsets, homeworkers, mobile devices, chat, e-mail, and the list goes on and on. It is ironic that with all this convenient technology, Customer satisfaction has steadily declined, at least in the minds of the Consumer. There are many reasons for this and ways that you can correct this in your own business. As more Customers have access to the web and the transactional information that can be found there, the likelihood that they will be calling about a difficult or unique situation increases. We discuss this over the next few chapters. But the first question you have to ask is whom do you trust with the keys to long-term business success?

When you look at your most senior level positions, do you have them handled by an outside firm or someone who has no direct correlation to your company or shareholders? Probably not. Yet we do this with some of the most powerful positions within our company. It is not uncommon to outsource your own Customer interaction.

When you call a business, can you tell if they outsource their Customer Service? What message does that send to you as a Consumer? Are you sending the same message to your own Customers?

You may be assuming by now that I am against outsourcing Customer Service. The answer is a little more complicated than that, and there are many circumstances in which it makes sense. It is just a question of how it is done where we can get into trouble. Thirty years ago, calls were much less complicated than they are today, yet many businesses fail to realize that. Prior to the implementation of technology, many of the interactions were routine and transactional in nature. You might have called your bank for your balance, where today you just log onto the website. Now when you actually call your bank it is much more detailed, such as trying to understand a transaction more deeply or discuss your full relationship so you have the best experience. So before making the decision to outsource, or even if you already have decided to outsource, start looking at why Customers are calling you in the first place. Is it transactional? The more intricate the call, the closer you must be to your Service team. This will help the business grow, and create the right experience for the Customer. Make sure your product leaders are working directly with those on the phones. The insights they gleam will help you improve the overall experience for your Customer and empower those talking to your Customer. If your business is too small to support hiring a Customer Service team, your best option may be to outsource. If you have to take this step, it is still imperative that you treat these outsourced agents as if they were part of your company. Encourage the same interaction model as if they were just outside your door. Listen to calls with them, and make them a key component of your feedback loop. Their work experience will reflect on your brand's reputation.

Amazon has always had an interesting take on Customer Service. They view any call as a failure of their website to be able to complete the task. They then use this call data and work to fix the underlying problem. This reduces their overall costs from a service perspective, but it also creates more positive Customer experiences. Years ago I experienced multiple issues with a rebate program that Amazon offered regularly. Each time I would have trouble obtaining the rebates that I believed I deserved. After hearing complaints through their service channels about the system, Amazon completely revamped the process with more automation. Amazon created a great experience by showing they were listening causing me to no longer have a need to interact with the service department again for any other reason. I have been a raving fan ever since. Not because they told me they changed, but because I personally noticed the difference.

In my experience, one of the best ways to improve Customer Service is by building direct relationships with the agents who serve your Customers. I have had the opportunity to do this with in-house teams as well as with outsourcers, although that is a little trickier. If you use offshore centers there are many cultural issues that you will have to understand and overcome in order to determine exactly what is happening each day. Just like internal centers, outsourcers will always put their best foot forward and prepare for visits, but the moment that you leave their world, it will return to exactly where it was.

Trust can be built the same way it is in any other relationship. It comes down to actions and approach. While I was at Advanta, we worked on offshoring some of our service functions.

I was part of a team challenged to create the same experiences we had with our internal teams with our outsourcer. We had high expectations, and we needed to find ways to overcome the common offshore experience.

First, we started with training. We knew that we had a unique company culture and it was imperative that others working for the organization knew that and participated in it, no matter where they lived or worked. We flew the offshore agents to Philadelphia for three weeks to learn from our teams in the same manner that our own employees learned. While they were in town, we shared experiences that showed the family nature of the organization, as well as our pride in our community and love for the humanities. During one of the visits, I even invited the team to my home for dinner. They actually returned the favor by again coming to my house and cooking a traditional Indian meal, which to this day remains one of the best experiences in my life. We were becoming family and that trust would translate deeply into the way we conducted business with them. As an organization we not only did this in training, but we also sent people to their cities to live.

Over time, I was able to speak directly with these same agents, asking questions and learning about their needs, the environment in which they were working, and ways we could improve the Customer experience. We then were able to utilize this information to drive change for the Customer and our team members working on the other side of the world. Some of the ways that we worked were very different from the top-down structure that they were accustomed to, but as time went on we saw Customer satisfaction rates equal to or sometimes even better than our U.S. teams. In assessing the situation I find it key to maintain your company's culture even in an outsourced environment and have a free flow of information with those who are closest to your Customer.

This is only one way to obtain information on what works best. Technology can also be utilized to stay close to the Customer wherever they are talking. One such technology I mentioned earlier converts words spoken in calls to searchable text. In working with outsourcers, we often used the same technology in order to provide a complete picture of the Customer experience no matter what center was handling the call. This allowed us to dig into topics and understand what we did well, and where we were failing. After reviewing numerous call types, I can tell you that our outsourced partners did very well with calls that were process driven. Calls that did not follow the process or were in a gray area, typically failed.

The closer watch you have on your Customer experience, the better you can manage where it should reside and who should be managing it. Customer Service is not as much of a process today as it once was, and part of success is recognizing that fact.

CHAPTER

21

Do You Trust Your Service Team?

Chris Brogan and Julien Smith, in their book *Trust Agents*, discuss in great detail what a trust agent is and the impact that trust agents have on the web. The book is concentrated on the external aspects of social media, but I would make the case that trust can come through in every interaction that your brand has with Customers. Your service personnel must be considered to be trust agents by the Customers they interact with. We tend to trust people we perceive to be like us.

In the service world, we have been afraid of showing emotion, yet the best calls demonstrate these emotions. How often are your employees willing to say, "I am sorry"? Unfortunately, in many companies, this is virtually never. We have become a very litigious society. This has impact on everything we do, and on the way that businesses operate. This of course adds to the lack of humanizing experiences that occur. One of the first unofficial rules that we were taught was the inability to say, "I am sorry."

I doubt that you will find an official memo anywhere that says not to do this. In fact, during my career I have looked for memos like this and have never found one. But the message is delivered clearly to our employees. Do you have e-mails that travel around the company with a line at the bottom referencing attorney-client privilege? This happens procedurally at larger firms, and I am sure at some smaller companies as well. When legal concerns arise we instruct our people not to talk about them or give a very rigid answer for them to provide to the Customer, from which they are not allowed to deviate. All of this sends messages to the team. One of those messages is that saying "I am sorry" is somehow admitting fault, when in reality it is connecting with the person on the line and letting them know that you understand where they are coming from. Always remember that how you communicate to your employees sends a message. Sometimes that message may be about risk, other times it could be about profits; the way that the message is received will impact how you treat your Customers, even if it never was intended to be that way.

Let's apply the chicken and the egg story. Did actual litigation lead us down this path or did our fear of litigation create an environment where the lack of connection to the Customer resulted in their wanting to sue? I am not sure I will ever be able to answer that riddle, but I do know that when people feel a human connection they are less likely to take legal action.

Anyway, I am getting away from the purpose of the conversation here. Trust is built through human connection, not process. Trust agents listen and understand what is being said and they offer real solutions. They feel comfortable relating to you one-on-one. During a call their sole attention is to the needs of that Customer. To reiterate, empowerment is the key method for a company to succeed, as we have seen with Zappos and Ritz-Carlton. Although your company may not be similar to either of these companies, it is still important to empower employees and it is still a powerful statement about the organization and how they trust their employees. In an ideal world all brands would use similar rules to those outlined in the book *The Nordstrom Way*. The first rule is to use your good judgment in all situations. The second rule simply refers you back to rule number one.

Now let's look for reasonable ways to build empowerment. The first question to ask is "How transparent are you?" *Transparency* is a buzzword associated with social media and many companies like to say they are transparent; but actually, they share very little internally, except with the most senior officials. It is important to make your team feel that they are a part of determining the direction of the business. Involve your service personnel in key decisions; ask them their opinion and how they think the Customer will react. Ask them to help with traditional business challenges. For whatever reason, there is a fear that sometimes involving teams, such as your service team members, will result in information being shared prematurely. I am not going to hide that this could happen, but I bet many, if they hired the right people, will find that the team members may have alternative solutions to the business problem that will end up being more effective. For example, when they are discussing cutting costs, often the conversation turns to employees because they are the most expensive part of a company's balance sheet. But, if you were to engage service personnel, you may find process flaws that can have the same effect. You may also find the next business idea that will drive further success for the business.

We should also communicate more information to our teams. Instead of dictating a new policy to the Customer Service team, have a discussion to share the why, how, and business impact for the change and ask for their thoughts in return. This will help gain greater buy in if the change is implemented. Otherwise, if it is dictated in the traditional manner, your service team, especially those really dedicated to the Customer, may feel like it is the company making their job more difficult or, even worse, the Customers. For employees to feel empowered they must be able to ask questions, especially why and what the benefit is. They also must receive a human answer back. Saying something like "This price increase is part of the value for our Customers" is not going to fly with the Customer or the agent. The key way to communicate is by explaining the business aspects; explain what can be done for Customers and the reasoning behind the decision. Then, have them try to help formulate how to discuss it with the Customer.

Over the years, I have been in meetings with people who were sometimes reluctant to speak on certain topics in my presence because I was known as the Twitter guy. It always amused me that they would not trust me to make a decision on what I would share and not share on the site. I then realized that we tend to have that same fear of our service representatives. We worry that if we share too much with them, they will tell our Customers. Treat them like adults and they will appreciate you and respect you for doing that. They may also have many other thoughts on achieving the same business results in a way that has more of a positive impact on the brand.

As they feel more of a part of the organization, service reps will exude that in everything they do! It will also be a way that they can build trust inside the organization allowing them the ability to further their career. It can be challenging for your front level employees to break into other areas of the business because they do not get highlighted to others easily and decision makers do not see them.

Overall, allow your employees to share the voice of the Customer from their perspective. This is something attempted by many companies but the effort often lacks the follow-through.

The best practice method is to allow the employee to share the feedback and then have executives from that business respond with their thoughts or ideas. This could be done through an ideation website, which is basically an internal version of My Starbucks Idea or Dell's IdeaStorm. These websites allow anyone to submit an idea and other users vote up or down the ideas. Some social media people will tell you that this is the future, although I tend to disagree with that, especially in respect to the Customer using it. It depends on the brand and the product if Customers want to define future innovation. The best way for businesses to use ideation websites is not focusing as much on the top voted items, but really reviewing all of the entries to find the hidden gem. The better sites, such as My Starbucks and Dell's IdeaStorm, as well as one run by Intuit, are exemplary because the people running them know that the best ideas are usually buried and they know how to pick them out and get them to the right people within the business. When used internally, it is sometimes easier to find these gems plus it allows people who really know the product to help define the future. When companies become really good at the implementation of ideas, using this concept externally can then be very useful. The challenge is not just creating the site, but the process as well to truly listen, locate the gems, implement them in a timely way, and follow through with those who presented the idea in the first place. Any way you engage your frontline employees will bring the voice of the Customer to the forefront of the conversation.

To recap, keys so far are giving your employees a say in your organization and showing trust in the way that you communicate to your employees. The third and final key to this puzzle is allowing your employees to make mistakes. We know the expression "Stuff Happens" (you may have heard a different variation), and this is especially true in the Customer Service field. Interactions are happening every day, and even if you are right 99.9 percent of the time, that one-tenth of a percent that you are wrong can be huge. Unfortunately, the typical Customer Service manager scolds those who made these mistakes instead of celebrating them as an opportunity to educate the agent, the team, or the business. In our existing metrics, we concentrate on the bad, bad agent instead of valued, valued employee. People will live up to the standards that you set in place and if you expect them to be the bad, bad employee, they will inevitably become just that. As we go into the next section, we focus on how to measure performance in your call center. Today's focus on poor metrics often sends the message to above average employees that they are bad. But as we make this shift to the relationship hub, we will then be celebrating our employees. This celebration will become contagious throughout the organization and to our Customers!

It will all start with hiring the right team members that embody what the organization is about, then trusting them to do the right things. When mistakes happen, celebrate them and learn from them. This is how we begin to build trust agents. At the end of the day, it is not our opinion that determines that they are in fact trust agents; in contrast, it is our Customer that sees them as trust agents. In building our relationship hub we need people whom we can trust, too. Leaders of the call center should be passionate for the Customer and their teams. They should be the type of person willing to share the good, the bad, and the ugly. These same attributes should flow through the management team. Agents should be well spoken, with the ability to think on their feet. You want them to understand the systems and how to best use them. More importantly you want people who can relate easily to your Customer. Hire passionate people who can grow with your organization but also want to see long-term success.

In addition to our effort to hire the right people (as opposed to warm bodies!), we need to refocus on retaining the best talent within the organization. As we reexamine how we educate our employees, we shift focus to develop skills beyond servicing Customers. Our goal is to help them learn long-term career-oriented skills that enable them to grow with the organization. I know many companies offer education reimbursement, and this has always been an admirable first step, but it is costly and lives are busy. You may not realize it, but many of your frontline employees work multiple jobs, or as much overtime as possible to simply support their family. Some have to rush home due to childcare issues and other commitments. Any time left is minimal and they may prefer to share that time with family and friends. One easy, inexpensive way to give your team access to learning materials is to create a company library to share works that would benefit your employees. Helping to sharpen employees' skills and educate them will send a clear message that their development is imperative to organizational success. You can build a dedicated, trusted employee base.

Today our interviews often focus on abiding by rules, attendance, and seeking those that could be labeled "easy to manage." Instead we should conduct behavioral-based interviewing looking for real-life experiences in relating to others and managing upward. If candidates cannot demonstrate this ability, they are probably not the right fit for you or your Customer. These are skills that work well with the Millennial Generation and their dedication to people. Once hired and trained the key is building productive, long-term relationships with your employees. These mutually beneficial relationships will instill a culture dedicated to winning for the business and your Customer. The values you display toward your employees will be seen during every Customer interaction. The relationship hub is built with the employee and Customer in mind.

CHAPTER

22

The Tail Wagging the Dog

We have heard all kinds of phrases to describe corporations, but the game is changing! Some may depict the shift as the leadership pyramid being flipped, especially with the millennial generations becoming such a key component to our team. But the change happening in our hyperconnected world seems much more dramatic. Like many changes in business this is just the pendulum swinging. Over the years I have seen the momentum shift for many aspects of business, but rarely, if ever, does the pendulum land right in the middle. Typically I find it going to extremes, and this feels like it will be one of those times too. The challenge is that this new power held by our Customers and employees seems far greater of a change then a simple flipping of the pyramid. I think a better analogy might be that the tail is wagging the dog.

Leadership of your organization is at the head, attempting to guide the organization, but the workforce behind is propelling the organization forward and hopefully guiding the leaders down the right path. Customers, which you hoped were the tail wagging happily away, now have the greatest amount of control. This shift will be empowering for some leaders, but I am sure there will be other leaders who will feel that the situation is downright hopeless.

Before we get into the changes to your overall organization, let's review what we have already discussed. Consumers in general are being bombarded with more content than ever. This includes sports, movies, television, YouTube videos, blog posts, tweets, Facebook posts, and a million other things. With all of this, trying to get a particular message through to them is extraordinarily difficult. Changes in technology (including connected phones, televisions, computers, tablets, and the list goes on and on) have also contributed to the content quandary. This technology helps to distract us even further, or sometimes it allows us to filter out unwanted messages, such as skipping past your message, just like the DVR helps us skip commercials.

Although we ask Customers to share positive information about our brands, they do so in a way that meets their needs, not necessarily ours. All our faults as a business are out in the open for the world to see. It is forced transparency! Customers often like to share weaknesses in our products (the best example was the iPhone 4 antenna issue). Brands everywhere are finding their Customer Service torn to shreds online. Alarmingly, this often makes much more entertaining content than anything we as an organization could ever hope to deliver. Customers are laughing and crying together, often directing negative attention to businesses like yours. It is all out there and all the advertising in the world will not change this fact.

Now is the time for you to make your choice. Many leaders will try to pretend social media will go away. They think that it is just a fad! I have heard that before. Not that long ago people thought computers would never take off in the home. I know I could not survive without one, can you? Having this opinion will not change the fact that Customers will be out there talking whether the business leaders like it or not. I hope that you will try to guide your organization into this new reality. Companies that choose to lead the way will have a window of opportunity to jump well ahead of competitors. In my view large organizations will be slowest, which will open the door for new competitors to dominate the Customer landscape that is now forming in this hyperconnected world.

Over the upcoming chapters I will provide some keys to help you through the transformation to the new relationship hub as we start to focus key parts of our organization on the Customer. The biggest change is how we communicate to our Customers and our employees. We are going to work to create this relationship hub right at the core of our business. It will feed our product teams, and our service team will become the focus so they can constantly feed the Customer's feedback to all levels and create change. We are learning to embrace the Customer as a key member of our team. Marketing and communications will partner with the service team in the same manner that they do with the product team today. They will work to create messaging that can resonate with our existing and prospective Customers, letting both know they are important and that as an organization you have a full understanding of their needs and you appreciate them.

This all sounds very basic, but this is not the business reality that we see today. Unfortunately we are not usually communicating outside of our silos and all levels of the organization struggle to align their own goals directly to the Customer. Our marketing is often directed toward prospective Customers with enticing deals that tell them they are special, but it sends a message to our existing Customers that they are not as important.

Recently, Facebook started to implement changes to the way they advertise for businesses. Now personally I have not seen any evidence that shows me that Facebook ads are effective in any manner. Of course that does not have to do with Facebook, as much as it is with the way in which people use the platform. The importance is the way that Facebook is changing ads, as well as the way business pages are shown, it is really about the Customer. Ads are about likes and comments from your fans. Would your Customers want to share their experience in that manner for you? My gut reaction when I saw the changes was that product companies will probably enjoy them, but service oriented business are in trouble unless the organization does a complete change in the way they treat its Customers. Customer stories will be the ads in the future, not just on Facebook but also in Internet searches. This shift is the tail wagging the dog and a key reason why your messages to Customers must be presented and interpreted in the right manner.

We have to get everyone in the organization on the same page. Many companies will start this with a mission or vision. Sometimes these statements look like pure fluff, usually written by someone in the Communications department for a nice external message for others to read. You have to know your company to determine if a mission or vision is important. I think they can be, but they have to be written with everyone in mind and those at the top of the organization must genuinely live them each and every day. It is imperative that the mission or vision become an integral part of your company culture at all levels. Then we must define the expectations that your business has for the overall Customer experience. Eventually this might take the form of a Customer guarantee. You are taking this opportunity to redefine to the Customer what they can expect from you.

The next key step is to consider creating some type of employee guarantee. Realize that all too often we are sending messages to the employees that they are not important to the organization. Many times we send messages to our employees that they are downright expendable. If you do not believe me, pull out your employee handbook and read a few of the rules. You may want to pay close attention to the employment at will section. That sends a very clear message! Now you can understand why employees often do not trust leadership of their company. Intentionally or unintentionally, you have been sending messages like this for years.

As we redefine Customer and employee expectations, it is crucial to review the measurements that we have in place for our teams. We have to start off with a few key metrics that should be on everyone's dashboard or scorecard. Clearly profitability, expense management, and revenue are imperative for any business, so of course we should start there.

One of the hidden ways in which companies are graded is reputation. If a business has a poor reputation, it is reflected in the share prices just like a positive reputation can have a multiplier effect on your stock. The problem within most companies is that people think only of the silo in which they work and do not concentrate on the overall reputation of the business. By concentrating on reputation metrics, you can begin shifting everyone's focus to building the brand. There are a variety of ways to measure reputation. One of the more common methods is looking at and analyzing your online reputation. Depending on the industry you are in, you can use many third-party companies or tools that already exist to measure online sentiment. I do not recommend using tools without understanding the data behind the measurement. The numbers will be skewed based on the tool and the sarcastic, snarky web. Tools struggle to measure things like "I love that company." Depending on context, that can be very positive or very negative. If you are a large enough company, using a third party, such as NM Incite for this is ideal.

If you use a tool, like Radian 6, in conjunction with a human to validate the positive or negative rating for each post, the person could have influence over the results. This may not be ideal for your company because of the false readings it can return or the time or cost required to obtain accurate numbers.

One of my favorite organizational metrics is something referred to as Net Promoter Score (developed by and a registered trademark of Fred Reichheld, Bain & Company, and Satmetrix). If you are not familiar with the name Net Promoter Score, you are certainly familiar with the survey question used to calculate it: "Are you willing to recommend us to a friend?" The scale is typically 0 through 10, with promoters responding 9 or 10 and detractors scoring 6 or below. To obtain the Net Promoter Score, subtract your detractors from your promoters. I do want to be balanced so I will also voice my frustrations with how it is often used, and the problem it poses to virtually every type of survey data. People like to use a number to compare other companies and industries. This sounds like a great idea, but there are many things that impact a Net Promoter Score and trying to make this type of comparison may not properly reflect your business. My preference is to use it as a means to follow the trend over time, specific to the company in question. Also remember that we have all been influenced by others to score surveys a certain way. When you buy a car, or sometimes take it in for service, you will be educated in advance on how to respond to the survey. One car dealer even had a picture of the survey and showed how you should respond. Once you begin to do these things, you may be helping your short-term results but over time you are also ruining the validity of the tool and the trend.

NPS results will start to guide conversations internally toward creating the right Customer experience through every interaction. Although this metric may be skewed toward brand reputation, it will serve as a greater guide to making sure everyone is focused on the Customer. Usually, if the survey is conducted frequently, it will be a strong early indicator of the direction in which your reputation is headed. Over the years, I have watched many organizations split apart internally because they were focusing on different goals or objectives, creating a divide in the brand. Too much disparity and a brand will cease to exist. In our hyperconnected world, concentrating on your brand reputation will increase sales and the willingness of your Customers to share their experiences with you.

Once you tailor NPS questions for your Customers, consider doing the same for your employees. Would they be willing to recommend your products? Would they recommend working at your company? NPS can be very versatile but the key is remembering that this is simply a trend. It is also important to know that managers may try to manipulate the numbers to benefit their own performance. If you build the right environment, you can work to mitigate this. I would also measure employee turnover and employees promoted into new roles. As you have success with these metrics, you will reap tremendous rewards with your reputational metric, and hopefully that will lead to greater profits and revenue!

As we redefined the goals of the organization, I am sure you have also realized that your relationship hub, centered by the Customer and powered by your Customer Service team, will need new metrics as well. We are going to shift your Customer Service center to many of the metrics I discussed in prior chapters. Gone will be things like handle time and quality. We will replace this with a Customer survey (similar to the NPS work the organization is doing), adherence to a schedule, and repeat calls. Many of the sales metrics will be removed, especially for our service personnel. We will have them focus on servicing the Customer, retaining Customers, and building the relationship. This focus will bring increased dedication from the Customer and therefore increased revenue possibilities.

When you go about implementing the survey, it is important to partner with your representatives and Customers to identify the best approach. Surveys should only be a few questions that are very easy to complete. It is important to also allow Customers the ability to input as many comments as they wish. The key is following up on all comments submitted. The timing of conducting the surveys should be based on Customer preferences, but also be careful that the results do not negatively impact agents when the cause is actually the company or process. Although many companies like to conduct the survey immediately following a call, in my experience immediate participation was skewed toward those who were most frustrated as a result of company decisions, not the overall interaction. Through the survey, ask specifically about the agent, but also ask about why the Customer called. When possible try to create a survey that incorporates related data already known, such as the reason for the call. If done right, this can be powerful information for all levels of your organization.

It is challenging to manage a call center, because you do need to make sure people are available when calls are coming in, so it would be important to measure adherence to schedule. The key to this is teaching your team why it is important and the benefits to them. Most call center agents do not fully understand what goes into effective scheduling, but they do understand the repercussions if people are not on the phones and should be. By positioning this right, there is immediate buy in.

It is important to work with your Customer Service professionals within your relationship hub to identify the best way to measure repeat calls. This will vary from business to business because the nature of the Customer calling patterns can vary widely. This measurement is powerful for the agent, but it is also a great way to help identify negative experiences created by processes or product flaws. Often people do not look at the costs generated by multiple calls, but they add up very quickly. This will be a key in our effort to reduce expenses for the organization while still improving the Customer experience.

We will also recognize and reward our Customer Service team for driving change upward and improving our products and ultimately increasing our revenue. Customer Service employees are a key component any organization's success and we will make sure the Service team fully understands how their role impacts that.

As we implement these changes, we also must focus our supervisors on the most important part of their job: their employees. No longer would the traditional call center turnover of 30 percent or more be acceptable. We would work to hire the right people and then create the right experience for them so they can grow their career within your company. This is a win-win situation for both the employee and the business. Not only is this building an organization focused on the Customer, it is also helping us create advocates for the brand.

In the relationship hub, Customers may be at the center, but we must recognize that our frontline employees have the keys. They can help deliver the Customer's story to all levels of the organization, drive change, and open the dialogue in insightful ways.

23

How Do You Speak?

We all have experience with pass it down the lane messaging. Inevitably the message is completely different at the end of the line. As we are realizing in the social web, and as you read about the call center, the messages that leaders are sending are not always the same ones resonating with the Customer or your service team. We need to fix this now! Our Customers need to hear the right message from executives, call center agents, and every employee within your company. The world is connected and they are listening to the signals you send.

Not all businesses have call centers, but all deal directly with some sort of Customer, whether it is business-to-business or business-to-Consumer. It is all the same and it starts with a relationship. As mentioned, the key is starting with hiring the right people and creating the best work environment for your employees. Do your employees have access to key decision makers within your business? Do they have access to each other? First, let's take a look at communication within your business. Most people will look at their business and say that they have excellent communication, but how is it actually being used? Is it an environment where the lowest level employees feel safe sharing ideas or feedback? In larger businesses this is the number one challenge as they often restrict access to some employees to things like e-mail or instant messenger. This is done often in production-type roles, such as Customer Service agents. It sends a clear message that their input is not valued and they are not trusted. If you feel that way, how would you treat your Customer? How would you treat the brand?

As we have seen around the globe, social media is helping to connect people in new ways. You may want to consider using external social media to connect to each other internally; a great first step would be implementing internal social media style tools to help connect your team. Imagine a world where an employee could send a short message, similar to a tweet, asking how to explain something to a Customer. Then another representative chimes in with the answer. That helps create a much better experience for all involved. I have discussed this in the past and a typical fear is that employees will share bad information on the platform. My response is emphatically "Good!" We are kidding ourselves if we think our employees are not sharing workarounds to processes or rules. Since the first-ever company brought on multiple employees, they have been sharing things. The benefit to facilitating this conversation is that you now can be a fly on the wall. If something is not being handled in the ideal manner, you can be part of the dialogue to fix it. The key is not disciplining the employee for being bad, because if you do, employees will not use the tool. Instead, teach them the business reason for the process and help them understand the why. Treat them like adults. It may seem silly to have to say that, but over the years I have seen poor managers handle these things in a substandard fashion, and as we already discussed, that can impact your brand internally and externally. Another side benefit of this internal platform is the efficiency of obtaining information in real time for both the business and the employee. Ultimately this dialogue can really help improve the employee and Customer experience.

Senior leaders should also be blogging internally regarding what they are working on and their overall vision. I am not suggesting that they share confidential information or that they share information prematurely. But keeping employees in the loop is a great way to get your team on the same page so you can work together toward a common goal. In addition, executives can have a dialogue with your team through the comments feature on the blog. These simple steps can help make the largest of organizations run like they are small and nimble by supplying a unified team-feeling within the company. Tools to bring these capabilities to your business are easy to obtain, and usually inexpensive. Many CRM systems have the tools built right into them, such as Chatter by Salesforce. Likewise, if you use Sharepoint for your internal intranet site, there are many tools similar to blogs, Facebook, and Twitter that are either built in or easily added through widgets. Beyond these, there are also many freeware options available on the Internet. There really is no excuse not to give this a shot.

Communication is key to brand success but it is also the key to winning with Customers. First, determine the types of communication that your Customers prefer. For some businesses, the phone may be the only method of communication necessary. If that is the case, build the best phone experience for your Customers. In other businesses, your Customers may have many preferences; so find ways to incorporate multiple channels effectively so that your Customer has the same great experience regardless of the channel. No matter how you interact, it is imperative to be able to monitor these interactions, not just for the business, but also for the Customer Service representative. If a Customer is interacting with your website, and then they pick up the phone, the agent needs to know specifically where they are on the website.

It shows that your business is connected and works as a team. Unfortunately, most companies view their website in a silo of technology or marketing, but it is really a Customer touch point in its own right.

Over the years I have had way too many interactions with doctors. Some experiences were amazing, yet others left a bit to be desired. When you call a doctor and make an appointment, the receptionist will ask you the reason for the visit. Then you go for the appointment and they have you fill out a bunch of forms, asking the same questions. Next, you are taken to a room and the nurse asks the same questions yet again. Then (and I have had this happen on multiple occasions) the doctor comes in and asks the exact same questions once again. Are they trying to see if I change my story?

This disconnect can be very frustrating, yet we do this to our Customers regularly. In the same way, the medical field could benefit from applying multiple channels for communication with their patients or Customers. Earlier this year, I was diagnosed with diabetes. This occurred during a regular checkup and was completely unexpected. I learned of my diagnosis when I received lab results in the mail along with a form letter stating that I have diabetes and another box checked off saying to call for an appointment. This would have been a circumstance in which I would have preferred a phone call, or at least a personalized letter. I had no way to communicate with this simple piece of paper and I felt frustrated. As I did not feel like I was a priority to them as their patient or Customer, I am no longer their Customer. This is an important lesson to take away when dealing with your own Customers.

Another disconnect I often see with businesses is the lack of follow through. A lack of communication sends a clear message. I always participate in surveys to share feedback, good and bad, with a company. Many times these surveys send a variety of messages. I recently took a survey for a major department store chain for an interaction I had on their website. The overall experience was not among the best I have had, which was surprising because the company prides themselves on service. The first question was the NPS survey I mentioned in a prior chapter. I rated the company zero, stating I would not recommend them. The very next question asked why I would recommend them. Huh? I just clearly stated that I would not. This simple error was making it seem like they were not listening to me. Later in the survey it asked if I wanted follow up, to which I stated yes (because an item was not included that should have been). I selected to have them follow up by phone. As of this moment I have not received a call. I did get a form e-mail stating that they hoped I would give them another chance. The funny thing with that e-mail is it seemed very personal, except it inputted my name in all caps (while the rest of the e-mail was normal writing) and it came from a no reply e-mail address.

Issues are going to happen, and if you follow the items outlined throughout this book, you will be able to identify those promptly and hopefully correct the organizational issues that created them in the first place. The challenge is building the right communications plan to follow through. Follow up is a key aspect to communications and Customer Service. This holds true no matter how you found out about the experience, whether it was a survey response, like the example above, through research using call recording equipment, social media listening, an e-mail to your executives, or simply an experience highlighted by one of your employees. Newer call recording equipment can even queue calls for management review where the Customer's tone indicates a possible problem. I mentioned earlier that a failure in service is not correcting the underlying cause of these issues. Another failure is not contacting the person back to apologize for the trouble and letting them know how it is being corrected. You have the opportunity to surprise and delight them by not only correcting the issue for them but also highlighting what the business is doing. This method of communicating sends a clear message that as a business you are focused on creating the right experience. It builds trust in future experiences.

Communications with Customers are key to building the right connection, but how you communicate is just as important. As I mentioned previously, when it comes to social media, people everywhere tell companies that they need to be on Facebook, LinkedIn, and Twitter. They will tell you that your Customers are there, so you have to be there, too. I disagree. People use these tools in specific ways and they may or may not have any interest in becoming your fan. Before spending money to develop these things, find out from your particular Customers how they want to communicate with you and what they really want from your business. There have been studies, including a recent one from Ehrenberg-Bass Institute that found only 1 percent of Facebook fans actually interact with brands. So why do they like companies? In a study by the CMO Council, the most common reason is to receive discounts. It is fascinating when contrasted with what marketers thought the reasoning was. Marketers believed it was because they were loyal Customers. If your Customers prefer fan pages or apps, then go for it, especially if you can offer them discounts. But if they do not want to communicate with you in that manner, do not push it. You can probably do other things that incorporate social media, such as offering the ability for visitors to your website to easily share your content to Facebook, Twitter, LinkedIn, Google+, and so on.

A better, more authentic, means to communicating about your brand on places like Facebook, LinkedIn, Google+, or Twitter, may reside with your own employee. Of course, even without your permission, this is done regularly. Our work life is a huge chunk of our day and we tend to share what is important to us. Take the time to teach your employees about the brand and what they can or cannot do in regard to mentioning the brand online. Let them shine! This can lead to internal changes where your organization uses the connections they have in the social media world to connect with people that are important to your business. For example, someone might have a connection at a firm that could benefit from your product, so working with that connection is a much stronger approach then a typical cold call.

I do think it will take time for organizations to loosen up and provide access to social media for employees, but the same fear and slow response happened with the introduction of the phone in the workplace. I am sure managers were afraid to place phones on desks because their employees might talk to family and friends all day instead of working. I know for a fact that the same reaction happened regarding e-mail (in fact it is still happening).

There are many other aspects to social media that you can consider adding to the Customer experience, but the same rules apply. A popular social media concept is building a forum that allows Customers to speak with other Customers. What is important to remember is that this will work only if Customers would want to hang out and talk about your products. I find that this channel is most effective for highly passionate products such as technology. Beyond that, it is often just hype. One failure I have seen with community forums is the inability to connect discussions within the forum to other Customer communications channels. It can be difficult for technology companies, such as a router company, to know every aspect of cable modem and computer configurations, but the answers to these issues can often be found in the forum. Other service personnel need access to this information and need to be able to utilize it during the calls. They can always say, "I do not have the answer, but in searching our forum, I found a great conversation on the topic." This also helps in guiding the Customer there for help in the future. It's a win-win!

Other popular discussion involves ratings and reviews. With so many sites already dedicated to this, would your Customer find value in this information directly on your website? Would they trust the information? Are product owners willing to accept negative commentary about their product on your web property?

Each way to connect with a Customer will vary; the key is finding what is best for your brand and your Customer. One great example is from Dish Network, the satellite TV provider. Charlie Ergen, the founder of Dish Network and current chairman, hosted a quarterly program called *Charlie Chat*. During the show, Customers would write in or call with questions. Questions could be on any topic and Charlie would do his best to answer. When I had Dish Network, I watched *Charlie Chat* every time that it was on. It was refreshing to see Charlie's response, particularly when he did not know the answer. He would be open about not knowing the answer, and then he would turn to his senior leaders who were always in the audience and put them on the spot. It was authentic and built up a huge trust for the brand. *Charlie Chat* was discontinued when Charlie hired a CEO in mid-2011 so that he could focus more on strategic direction for the company. Today, a business could do something similar using YouTube, Facebook, or Google+. You could even do a question-and-answer session on Twitter. Customers love authenticity and access.

Communication is key to success in today's world. Know how your Customers want to speak with you and strive to deliver on that. At the same time there is no need to add other means to communicate that will not be seen as beneficial for your Customer. Understanding communication will be key with your relationship hub!

CHAPTER
24

Startle Your Customer

In the world of Customer Service we often talk about startling our Customers in a positive way. Of course in recent years companies have startled their Customers with the poor service they provided. In a social world, we are being forced to change that and build experiences that will create loyalty, dedication, and positive buzz. So as we work to gain social media success, we will deliver an amazing product and start to create Customer interactions to help facilitate positive buzz. This is easy since Customer expectations are at a low, but as this improves, the next step will be taking it to another level.

Since expectations of service are so low, you can often startle your Customer just by following up on feedback to say thank you or we hear you. This can always be shocking and completely change the impression of the company. In 2010, I received one of those insurance explanation of benefits forms. You probably have seen them, and if you are like me, just ignored them or placed them in a drawer. This time it was different. The form had my deceased daughter, Gianna, listed as the subscriber. Needless to say, that got my attention. Gia passed away in 2004, and at no time was she ever listed on that insurance policy. As you can imagine I called immediately, but that did not provide any explanation or hope of resolution, so I e-mailed the president of the company. The response was amazing! First the president responded to my e-mail directly with a personal apology. He was obviously horrified with the error. The company went many steps further. They FedExed a very detailed letter fully explaining the exact cause of the system generated error, exactly why the agent could not see the issue when I called, and very detailed steps they were taking to ensure not only that this could not happen in the future, but also how they would improve their agent experience to better assist a Customer in a similar circumstance. Included with the package was a handwritten note from the president apologizing again and offer any assistance in the future. This was well above and beyond, and it startled me.

Years ago I had an issue with a bank and when I shared feedback with them, they surprised me by sending me a Peace Lily with a note saying they would call me the next afternoon. I had already closed out my account, but after receiving the plant, by the time they called I was very willing to reopen the account. Although today I do work for a competitor, the Peace Lily is still alive and I think fondly of the experience. I maintained a relationship with them for years after that incident. I would like to think in a perfect world we could make sure negative experiences like the one with the insurance company or the one with the bank would never happen, but that is just unrealistic. It is imperative that we learn the right way to apologize when these missteps occur. Apologies in any form can be very powerful and long lasting, like the Peace Lily. Of course we should not wait for the negative experience to be the only reason we startle our Customers!

If you tweeted out to a restaurant, asking them to meet you at the airport with a steak when your plane lands, would you expect it to happen? Is it realistic? It actually did happen when Peter Shankman, author, speaker, and entrepreneur, sent a tweet out to Morton's. To Peter's surprise, Morton's met him at Newark International Airport with a porterhouse. According to Peter, this was not a PR stunt, as many would believe. I am sure the fact that Peter is the author of *PR Stunts That Work and Why Your Company Needs Them*, added to this perception. Instead Peter viewed it as good Customer Service. Of course the nearest Morton's, according to Peter's blog post, was 23 miles away. Peter may be an amazing Customer, but I am sure Morton's is not in the habit of delivering food at that distance. Ultimately, whether planned or not, this was PR that certainly created discussion for their brand. It also stirred conversation questioning whether they would do that for the ordinary Customer or just for Peter based on his book or 100,000 followers. This type of effort, although interesting and possibly viewed as Customer centric, would be difficult to scale and doing it regularly would minimize the impact. It also has the risk of sending a message to other Customers telling them they are not as special. Of course I am now craving a Morton's steak and potatoes, but I doubt I could convince them to bring it to me, so it will have to wait for another day. If you do try this with them, or another restaurant chain, and it is successful, please let me know! I would love that story.

Zappos has often found ways to surprise their Customers. For example, they often offer upgraded shipping at no additional charge after you have made your purchase. Shortly after placing your order you may see an e-mail with the headline: "Good News Regarding Your Zappos Order." They will surprise and delight you as they tell you that your order will arrive sooner than expected. They say, "It's kind of like we waved our magic wand!" This is just one way that they thank their Customers and show them how much they are valued.

How does that make you feel? Certainly it adds to the experience of being a Zappos Customer and makes you want to consider them for other purchases. Zappos also offers free return shipping and, if you are conducting an exchange, they will often send out the new shoes at the same time, so you will not have to wait. That is how you create a wow experience.

Zappos also builds the emotional connection with their Customer by remembering events, such as when you bought a pair of shoes or your anniversary with them. I recently received e-mail from Zappos with the subject line of "Celebrations Are in Order." The body of the e-mail included an unusual, catchy three-year anniversary jingle to show their appreciation. These e-mails reinforce the culture of Zappos and build on their core values. They may not be ideal for your business, but the idea here is to help generate thoughts for you to wow your own Customers.

One of my favorite methods was something we did at Advanta, designed to startle our Customers. We would purchase blank Hallmark cards with a nice picture on the outside and nothing on the inside. Our representatives, when appropriate for the situation, would send their Customer a handwritten card. It would be an apology, congratulations, or anything else that was fitting to the conversation they had just had. Representatives were empowered to send cards to Customers as they saw fit. It always surprised Customers to receive them. We also empowered our employees to send flowers if appropriate. They could send something up to $25 (more with approval) from a local florist that we worked with. Employees had a limit per month and they were taught to use it wisely. When Customers opened these greeting cards or received these floral arrangements, they were always startled, hence the name we provided to the program. It is not what people have come to expect from a credit card company and it made us stand out.

There are many ways to help your brand stand out; some are easier than others. Proactively calling a Customer to say hi, without trying to sell them can be startling. Using information you already have and incorporating that into the experience is startling. This could be as simple as wishing someone a happy birthday when they call near that time. As we discussed in Chapter 10, we now have the ability to build intimate connections with our Customer. Acknowledging success in their life or expressing sorrow for some of the negative aspects in life can go a long way. We have the opportunity to show how human we are, and our business can play a role in that. The personalized experiences that are now possible will change the game. It may be a simple hand-written note, or saying happy birthday or letting them know you are thinking about them during a difficult time. The world is very different now, and with all the information we have at our fingertips, we have the ability to really build personal relationships at scale. It will not take hand-delivering steak to your Customers at the airport (although I will welcome that any time!), but it will take communicating to your Customer that you do understand them and their needs.

CHAPTER

25

Responding to Social Media Crisis

Since the dawn of the Internet, businesses have had to deal with a variety of unexpected events hurting their brand image. What was once governed by the 24-hour news cycle is now almost immediate. For the PR professional, crisis management is reinventing their role in the organization. This is not all that different than what your Customer Service teams deal with every day! There is a lot PR professionals can learn from service, and vice versa. But, in my view, the crisis is greater than these groups even imagine. Depending on your brand, conversations all over the web are becoming critical to your brand. They influence prospective Customers or employees searching out their next career move. This, in many ways is a revolution against brands. With this shift in control, we have to learn better, more creative, ways to be part of the conversation.

What can a company do? How can you defend against that? What do you say? The only way to truly fix and then prevent against these external issues is to fix the underlying problems that may exist within your company, allowing you to slowly mend your reputation. There are companies that will sell you a quick fix in reputation management, but often what they are really doing is manipulating data or search results, not truly fixing the underlying cause. So how do you deal with this type of commentary?

Social media crises can be very unique in comparison to traditional crisis management. Speed has always been important, but now speed of response is critical. With the introduction of Twitter and other online platforms, commentary is much more instant and it can proliferate across the web in seconds. The key to your response is to be as human and as transparent as possible and do so as quickly as possible. At first you may respond with "we are looking into this and we will update you as soon as we have more information." If dealing with an upset Customer, do not be afraid to be humble or say that you are sorry and let them know you want to help. If it is a disgruntled employee, guide the conversation offline as soon as possible, but do not be too harsh. Listen to the concerns; most likely they were just trying to send a message. Sometimes they are just living their passion for the brand, which if guided properly, can be a huge asset.

Over the years I have dealt with a share of social media issues, especially those related to Customers. I have found that the more human you are, the faster you can turn it around. During one noteworthy experience, because it involved Customers, we were talking about it from the moment it happened. We then continued to update as we learned more about the cause of the situation. We shared as much as we could everywhere we saw discussion. One of the websites, which typically did not like the brand, posted something like some "hapless PR sap left us this message." So when I came back I wrote, "Hey this is the hapless

PR sap. I actually work in Customer Service, but I promised an update and here it is." After that response the audience for that website was easily won over. In another example I noticed an employee tweeting about not wanting to go to his work location. I did not berate him, but I did respond refocusing the comments on traffic in that area. In a subtle way this let him know to be careful about what he presents via social media. I have also dealt with a variety of issues involving controversial videos with an inappropriate message regarding the brands I worked with. During one of these incidents, instead of disputing the video, I played it to a crowd while speaking at a social media event. They were shocked at the openness. I then played another video, also from YouTube, that was produced by the same people as the other video. This new video provided clarity to what really transpired and the audience helped take my message to the Internet for me. The online discussion changed almost immediately. Let's look at a few other examples.

Our first involves Motrin, a product of McNeil Consumer Healthcare, a Johnson & Johnson company. If you remember back to the cyanide scare for Tylenol years ago, J & J was a case study on the best ways to handle product crises.

Back in 2008, the Motrin team created an ad discussing ways people held their babies and the pain it often caused. As you may have guessed, mothers reacted to this and took to the social web to voice their opinions. Twitter was a powerful platform for them: One mom put a very powerful video together featuring tweets and pictures of their babies. As a result of this backlash, McNeil Consumer Healthcare pulled the ad and placed an apology on their website. Ironically, more people probably saw the apology than saw the original video. Imagine if McNeil employees just tweeted back to the first tweets, thanking the mothers for their feedback and assuring them that their thoughts would be shared with the leadership team. There is a lot to learn here, particularly the benefits of listening and engaging people early in the process. McNeil missed these opportunities. Companies also fail in their effort to be more transparent by then broadcasting the message to more people than would have ever seen this video in the first place. I do agree that pulling the ad was a great idea. I would have also recommended that a video response posted on YouTube would have been enough. By posting directly on your website, you are now highlighting the issue to potentially millions of other Customers who did not even know it was an issue.

Verizon Wireless is another interesting example. On December 29, 2011, Verizon Wireless announced a new fee for making single payments in a press release titled: "Customers Encouraged to Use Options to Avoid Single Payment Fee." (I do wonder if they timed the press release with the often-slow news cycle between Christmas and New Years, but social media does not have a slow news cycle!) Anyway, the press release outlined that the new fee was to help offset costs associated with single payments (as opposed to auto pay). In the press release, Verizon also outlined many ways to avoid the fee, including using electronic checks, making automatic payments, paying at a Verizon Wireless store, or mailing a check or money order. Despite the slow news cycle, the story took off in social media. One day later, Verizon reiterated that the fee would be instituted as the conversations about the brand continued. The FCC then chimed in, stating that they would look into this new procedure. By the end of the day on December 30, 2011, a new press release was issued with the following statement:

> Verizon Wireless has decided it will not institute the fee for online or telephone single payments that was announced earlier this week.
>
> The company made the decision in response to Customer feedback about the plan, which was designed to improve the efficiency of those transactions. The company

continues to encourage Customers to take advantage of the numerous simple and convenient payment methods it provides.

"At Verizon, we take great care to listen to our Customers. Based on their input, we believe the best path forward is to encourage Customers to take advantage of the best and most efficient options, eliminating the need to institute the fee at this time," said Dan Mead, president and chief executive officer of Verizon Wireless.

To their credit, Verizon did respond promptly. Was this response driven more by the online feedback or the fact that the FCC planned to look into the decision? In any event, the speed in which they made the decision not to implement the fee was impressive. In my view, the fee, if implemented, attempted to drive Customers to make automatic payments, and it is a logical supposition that auto pay Customers have higher retention rates and lower costs in terms of servicing. The individual transactions themselves do not have higher costs, so it seemed as if the fee was designed to change behavior. But is that the message to send to your Customers? If you were a Customer, how would you feel? The key message that you can learn from this story is the many people and organizations, including government entities, are now listening to online conversation. This will spur action from Consumers, but potentially others as well. Prior to releasing this type of information, you may want to test the best methods for presenting the new information. You must decide if the fee income it is producing is worth the negative reaction to the brand.

Domino's Pizza has done a number of impressive things within social media, but the first time I noticed them online was after viewing a not-very-flattering video created by employees at one of their franchises. The CEO did an amazing job to combat this criticism by responding with a video of his own, one in which he appeared sincere and human. Since that time, Domino's has embraced many aspects of social media and even utilized it as a marketing tool while they created a new pizza formula. Because of this the CEO won trust for the company on so many levels, something for which we all strive. Another important aspect to Domino's successful response was sheer speed. In the fast-paced nature of the web, the quicker you respond, the more likely you will be able to mitigate long-term pain.

Even prior to social media, we have seen the same formula prove successful for companies in trouble. One of the most notable examples is Lee Iacocca at Chrysler. He is widely credited with turning Chrysler around, but even more important than that, he was able to obtain widespread public support for government assistance as well as gain general public support for Chrysler itself while he tried to turn around the brand. It is not too often that we see the public cheering for companies like this one, but they were not doing it for Chrysler as much as they were doing it for Lee Iacocca.

This is the main reason I am a big believer in teaching your employees to use social media as it relates to your brand. Ultimately, they can build trust and earn respect in the space. They can also showcase your company and the good that it does in a believable manner. When something bad happens within a company, it is hard to believe the brand itself when they respond. But, I will believe an employee that I trust. Through their own interactions employees can build trust with existing Customers, and help you win new Customers.

At the same time, if employees are not taught how to deal with situations properly, their passion for your brand may drive them to represent the message of your brand in ways that you did not intend, as can be seen in the Kotkin example.

In this heated situation, I would have recommended that the company create a video personalizing the brand and exciting that passion within their Customer base. Next I would share the video in places that were already having the discussion on the topic. Video is a great way to excite people and to link positive images with a brand. The next step would have been to sever ties with the marketing firm that blemished the brand originally. They then should have assessed the conversations that were already taking place, analyzing who was participating in them and what was being said.

One problem with something going viral is that people around the web start picking apart the company at every angle. To combat that, companies must move past simply tracking the different discussions and decipher what exactly is being said. Often, companies strive to say the bare minimum in response to Customer complaints and backlash, but unfortunately, that can feed the fury and cause individuals to keep digging deeper into the company, thus damaging the brand even more. In the Kotkin situation, they had chaos: An employee started commenting, the former marketer was still out talking about what had happened, evidence of manipulated reviews for their product appeared, plagiarism on the marketer's website was discovered, alleged steroid use and prior arrest involving the marketer was uncovered, and the list goes on and on. All this came to light in about a span of twenty-four hours. Once your brand is embroiled in something like this, and trust erodes, anything can be questioned, and issues not relevant to the original situation come under fire.

The new PR representative for Kotkin Enterprises, once authorized, started tweeting with those talking about it. His responses had a very human, humble tone. He then started to use these conversations to help spread the press release so that it could best be seen by the gamers who were the most upset by this ordeal. The press release is interesting because it covers almost all aspects of the online conversation, effectively calming down the viral spread. Here is a copy of the press release for you to peruse:

DATE: December 28, 2011
CONTACT: Moisés Chiullan
E-MAIL: AvengerDefender@gmail.com

*** FOR IMMEDIATE RELEASE ***

AVENGER CONTROLLER DISMISSES MARKETING CONSULTANT, TAKES BACK MARKETING AND SALES OPERATIONS

Miami, FL—Wednesday, December 28, 2011—N-Control, makers of the Avenger Controller accessory, have categorically dismissed third party contractor [REDACTED NAME] and his marketing operation, known alternatively as Ocean Distribution or Ocean Marketing. This separation from Mr. [REDACTED NAME] extends to all business interests of N-Control, its founders, and its officers. Mr. [REDACTED NAME] does not and never did own, in whole or in part, a stake in N-Control LLC nor its affiliated companies (Kotkin Enterprises, iControl LLC).

Following the publication of an e-mail chain between Mr. [REDACTED NAME] and one of N-Control's Customers, punctuated by Mr. [REDACTED NAME]'s acknowledgment of his conduct, N-Control immediately proceeded to extricate Mr. [REDACTED NAME]'s access to their e-mail and social media accounts, a process that is still ongoing. In the interim, a Gmail address and Twitter account (AvengerDefender@gmail.com and @AvengerDefender, respectively) have been set up for press inquiries and Customer Service needs.

David Kotkin, the inventor and founder of the Avenger Controller, created the product to help one of his students who had a physical disability. The student wanted to play games the way that everyone else could. The Avenger evolved from a homemade solution for a deserving child into an even more sophisticated controller accessory, capable of enhancing even the most skilled gamer's performance.

"Everyone deserves the opportunity to be a part of the gaming community in a fun, positive way," said David Kotkin, Avenger founder. "I created the Avenger to make people happy. I deeply regret that so many people have any negative feelings toward it as a result of what has happened, especially since I've seen firsthand what an impact it can have on gameplay."

Kotkin continued, "What I'm most concerned about is doing right by our Customers. We have dropped the ball by giving them delivery estimates that did not come through as expected. We didn't expect that the demand would be so great, and we should have done a better job communicating that. Our new team is taking all necessary action to correct that going forward. I hope that people will give us a chance to earn back the faith they may have lost."

All existing orders will be honored, and PS3 Avenger pre-order Customers will all be extended the same $10 discount that some have already received. To clarify, Customers who have already received $10 off their pre-order are not eligible for an additional discount. N-Control agrees with "Customer Dave" that all of our PS3 early adopters deserve to be rewarded for their trust in the Avenger.

N-Control would like to publicly apologize to existing and potential Customers, as well as the gaming community at large, for allowing Mr. [REDACTED NAME] to abuse his power so unforgivably. The Avenger was invented to provide greater accessibility to disabled gamers, and bullying tactics are the last thing that should be associated with this product.

In the effort to dispel various misconceptions that have been forwarded via news reports and social media,

N-Control is offering the following clarifications on a variety of subjects:

N-Control has hired an independent consultant, Austin, Texas-based Moisés Chiullan (@moiseschiu), to field press inquiries and oversee sales and marketing operations going forward. They ask that Customers and the press alike bear with them as they field the tens of thousands of e-mails and other messages that N-Control has received. It is his intent that N-Control should respond personally to everyone who has e-mailed the info@avengercontroller.com address regarding this situation.

"We have to move forward and take care of Avenger's Customers," Chiullan said. "I can't worry about the fact that there isn't a bus big enough for me to throw [REDACTED NAME] under. The internet did that for me. I think they set him on fire too." He continued, "I just hope that people will have the common decency to leave his wife and child out of all this. They didn't send those e-mails, [REDACTED NAME] did."

All PS3 Avenger pre-orders are currently slated to ship by January 15 at the latest. Some orders will ship in advance of January 15. In consideration of the events of the past two days, N-Control ask[s] their Customers to bear with them as they sort out updating individual order estimates. General updates regarding shipping will be regularly delivered to Customers starting next week.

At no time during his tenure with N-Control did Mr. [REDACTED NAME] have direct access to Customer credit card information. N-Control does not retain any Customer credit card data for online orders, which are all processed via Google Checkout or Paypal.

Ocean Marketing aka [REDACTED NAME] owns no stake in the Avenger Controller nor N-Control, and does not stand to profit from further sales of the device either through N-Control or authorized resellers.

Contrary to how Mr. [REDACTED NAME] may have presented events (in public or private), N-Control never directly endorsed nor had knowledge of his communication with Customers in the manner found in his correspondence with "Customer Dave," who still wants his Avengers, despite everything that has transpired.

Steps have been taken to ensure that all future Customer communication is transparently visible to management at N-Control. N-Control regrets sincerely that the trust they placed in Mr. [REDACTED NAME] was so abused and betrayed and, as a result, may have tainted their reputation with existing and potential Customers and partners.

Regarding "Afternoon Artists," a company registered with the Florida Division of Corporations that lists [REDACTED NAME] as Treasurer, N-Control has the following statement: "This secondary business has never so much as opened a bank account, much less operated in any form outside of paperwork being filed. It was originally intended that Mr. [REDACTED NAME] would serve as an investor in this company, which, again, has never operated in any capacity, nor will it in the future."

N-Control employs [REDACTED NAME] as a part-time Social Media Consultant. He is an enthusiastic high school student who became one of the Avenger's earliest super fans, meeting the founder at a trade show. Mr. Kotkin is proud to encourage the development of a bright, enthusiastic young person like [REDACTED NAME].

[REDACTED NAME] is not, however, in charge of Marketing or PR for N-Control. Previous news reports have credited him as Marketing Manager, a title [REDACTED NAME] gave himself without the consent or advance knowledge of N-Control management. This occurred during the period of greatest upheaval following Mr. [REDACTED NAME]'s dismissal, and N-Control regrets that this mixed messaging reached the public. All press inquiries and media requests should instead be directed to Moisés Chiullan at the AvengerDefender@gmail.com address.

Contrary to rumors and speculation, [REDACTED NAME]'s Twitter account is his own and not controlled by [REDACTED NAME (the marketer)]. [REDACTED NAME] is a minor, and consequently, N-Control would appreciate the press and the public's discretion in their dealings with him.

For the foreseeable future, N-Control's official Twitter account will be "@AvengerControl", as N-Control does not have access to "@NControlAvenger". N-Control is not responsible for the content of any Twitter feeds associated with [REDACTED NAME].

For the foreseeable future, N-Control requests that Customers discontinue use of the toll-free phone number displayed on the AvengerController.com website, as well as any other means of contact found there. Instead, Customers should direct communication to AvengerDefender@gmail .com. They ask for patience due to the events of the last two days. Keep an eye on @AvengerControl on Twitter for updates.

For more details regarding N-Control and Avenger Controller, contact press agent Moisés Chiullan, at
        AvengerDefender@gmail.com.

For more information, follow Avenger Controllers on Twitter: @AvengerControl.

The press release covered most of the conversation that was taking place online and it did so in a very human way. Moisés Chiullan, the new PR representative, then took the conversation to where the Customers, and gamers, already were talking about the topic. This included offering interviews to popular gaming websites, following up existing blog posts, tweeting to those talking, and doing a Reddit "Ask me Anything." Reddit is a news discussion website and many popular news items gain popularity there. Users vote up and down news items while they add to the discussion and a Reddit AMA is a place where Reddit users can ask any question related to the topic. Moisés did a great job in answering questions openly and rebuilding trust with this very difficult, highly passionate audience. Throughout the question and answer, Moisés was able to personalize Kotkin Enterprises, separating them from their former marketer and truly presenting himself as one of them. It will be interesting to continue to follow Kotkin Enterprises as they come back from this unfortunate mishap. The web discussion has died down for now and I hope that they are able to prove that taking the right steps during a disaster like this can lead to a stronger business going forward. I am also hopeful that this scenario and how it was handled will prove to be a learning experience for other businesses.

Crisis is ubiquitous in this social media driven world and the way we handle it is key to our brand reputation. Similar to Customer Service interactions, it requires a personal, human touch and speed. The good news is there are many examples to help business leaders to learn from. The bad news is, with recent examples mentioned in this chapter, such as Netflix and the Verizon fee, as well as many others, including the Bank of America debit card fee fiasco (I skipped this because of my associate with Citi, but it would be interesting for you to Google), Customers have realized the monumental power they now have and will seize it. I expect this will grow in the coming years. Be prepared!

CHAPTER
26

Doing Social Good

We all love to hear about good things happening in our communities and our world. As Customers, we are proud when companies that we do business with are giving back to these communities and helping those in need. For example, Hyundai's efforts to help kids fight cancer through their Hope on Wheels program are close to my heart, so I often choose to speak about them. My admiration for Hyundai as a brand has increased because of this program.

Many businesses have built successful social media programs centered on helping the community. One of the most notable examples is the Pepsi Refresh Project. Started in 2010, Pepsi Refresh awards millions of dollars in grants to individuals, businesses, and non-profits that promote new ideas to help the community or society as a whole. They then ask their website and social media viewers to vote on the best ideas. Based on these results, Pepsi's marketing team then funds the winners. We have seen similar social media campaigns, like the Chase Community Giving Campaign, where users vote for the organizations or individuals who most deserve funds. This is a great way to help spread your brand message, while helping the community at the same time. It also often spurs the non-profit organizations to excite their own communities to visit the page and vote up their causes. Positive brand message can spread rapidly!

The challenge is that when we see successes like these examples, many other companies follow suit. Although that is not a bad thing, from a marketing perspective, the multitude of companies portraying community-driven messages can take away from the brand message that companies are trying to present.

Consumers should also remember that many companies elect to do their community efforts privately, with their employees, directly in the community with the people they serve. While these are certainly worthwhile efforts, think of it as an opportunity to share your actions with your Customers. While they might not be participants, they can still connect good feelings with your business.

If you do not decide to invite the community to join in your efforts, encourage your employees to speak about all the good that they are doing. Many companies have community service days, or sometimes set days or special time off so that employees can serve the community. If your employee is already participating in social media, encourage them to talk about the experience and invite their friends to join them. It becomes a very powerful statement for the brand and one that employees will want to share.

For those who work in the non-profit industry, social media is a great way to increase awareness for your message. First, your employees are already among the most passionate for any brand. There is a reason why they work for you, and it is usually not the money. They share your passion. The challenge for many non-profits is properly tapping this passion as well as the passion of your supporters, or "Customers." If you think of your supporters as your Customers, you can think of ways to reach them more easily.

One of my favorites charities is Alex's Lemonade Stand Foundation. Alex was only eight years old when she passed away from childhood cancer, but in her short life, she paved the way toward impacting millions of people, and continues to do so every day. Basically, Alex wanted to raise money for her doctors to help other children. Shortly after her fourth birthday, Alex held her first lemonade stand, raising $2,000 for "her hospital." She continued to hold her stand annually to raise funds for childhood cancer. At the time of her passing, she and others had raised over $1 million for this important cause. Today, Alex's legacy continues to grow through the Alex's Lemonade Stand Foundation. Jay Scott (@LemonadeJay on Twitter), Alex's father, leads the effort and is extremely appreciative of his volunteers. Jay's passion is fueled by the inspiration that he gets from kids with cancer.

Alex's Lemonade Stand Foundation believes that every person can make a difference in the world. When you talk to volunteers, they are motivated by the experience and their interaction with Jay and Liz, Alex's parents. Their passion permeates everything they do, creating positive brand image and helping forge connections with their supporters. They do not pressure volunteers: They treat them just as you would want to be treated, with respect and gratitude. In social media, Alex's Lemonade Stand does not push their message constantly, but instead they talk to people and share stories. They profile childhood cancer heroes, they personalize their team and the families whom their work supports, and they focus on their supporters. On their website, Alex's Lemonade Stand Foundation defines their presence in social media:

> We believe it's important to stay closely connected to our supporters and what better way than through social media! We're constantly posting updates online and communicating with our wonderful supporters. Please consider finding us on the following social media websites to stay up-to-date and connected!

Enhanced by social media, Alex's vision is now global. The foundation focuses on supporters and not forcing you to connect with them. In return they have more than 50,000 followers on Twitter, rivaling many for-profit businesses, and 85,000 fans on Facebook.

While I was at Comcast, I was pleased to be part of many initiatives to help charities, including a company-sponsored event hosted to help non-profits better use social media. During the Comcast New Media Exchange event, Jay Scott and I interviewed each other on stage! Through that event we were able to help many charities with their efforts.

Comcast also did a great job encouraging, but not forcing, employees to participate via social media during their annual Comcast Cares Day. This is a company-wide event where thousands of Comcast employees, friends, and family volunteer to help out in communities where Comcast serves. A pad of paper from this event, and that served as inspiration for the Comcast Cares Twitter handle I used for many years. In 2011, more than 70,000 employees, family members, and friends participated at over 600 locations in 39 states. They would make sure that employees could easily share pictures, post videos, and tweet. On those days, they were able to encourage others to participate with them, support some of their causes, and gain a better understanding of how much their employees care for the community in which they live. It is because of events like these that employees are proud of where they work and are able to demonstrate that passion to others.

It does not matter whether you are a business or a charity; at the end of the day, people do like to share good things about the organizations that they care about. Conversations centered on charitable acts, donations of time, resources, and money, philanthropic endeavors, benevolent acts, and unselfishness of businesses and employees can have an enormously positive impact on your brand. The bottom line is adding a human element to your brand, something that can be accomplished through altruistic examples.

CHAPTER

27

Scale of Change

The scale of change, especially for larger business, can be very overwhelming. Not only do you need to deliver shareholder value, profits, and all of that, but you also need to ensure a positive and attractive brand image, which has grown even more challenging due to social media. The message that you have been sending out via traditional marketing channels is no longer enough, or even resonating at all. Customers have gained control over brands, and now employees have an outlet for taking control of your brand, too.

In recent years, there has been a lot of discussion regarding who owns social media, PR or Marketing. I used to respond jokingly that Customer Service should own it. In reality Customers and employees own your social presence and they define your message. Now suddenly you have to worry about all of this and achieving results. No wonder many people just say, "Forget about it" and continue their same old way of doing business.

The problem is that we often wait until it is too late. Think about companies that you have done business with over the years that have gone by the wayside. In your view why did they disappear? Often it is because they did not properly shift with changing market conditions.

We are seeing more than the simple convergence of Marketing and PR, we are seeing the entire organization coming together or a flattening that is not as much about roles as it is about the way we conduct business. It is going to require strong leadership to help to unite and get everyone on the same playing field; it can be done. Start by determining what the objectives of your organization are. Also determine what values you want the world to know. Then make them a part of everything that you do throughout the company. Strong leadership in this area will be imperative to spreading a brand message. When Starbucks met challenges a few years back, the first thing that they did was work to return to the heart of the brand. Then they worked tirelessly to make it consistent through every Customer touch point. When all employees are on that same page, it does not matter where the interaction is; your business will exude those values.

The changing communication style will be difficult for certain segments of your work force, especially those more familiar and comfortable with a traditional top-down approach. It will also be a challenge for some leaders not to want to take a heavy hand with someone who is constantly speaking up. Work with the vocal employee and learn more about the root cause for their frustrations. Then have an open dialogue with them regarding the root cause. Hopefully, by doing this, you will teach the vocal employee more about the organization and even further ignite their passion, while doing so in a brand-positive manner.

We will also see some of the challenges occur in terms of how we portray the brand publicly, whether it is in the press, to our Customers, or our own employees talking. Releasing some of that control and having faith that the values you built will take hold is a shift in mind-set. Beyond that shift social media opens the possibility that an employee will build a bigger brand than the company. This is a topic that I planned to avoid, but it is the number one challenge with this shift. This is not very new, but it is becoming broader in the social world. David Alston from Radian 6 has built a large fan base over the years. When I was at Comcast I built a large following for the @ComcastCares Twitter handle. Who should own the fans? My perspective is that the fans should really be the ones to decide and that companies place too much emphasis on fan counts as opposed to focusing on ways to build true fans. From a legal perspective it is easy regarding @ComcastCares; it is Comcast.

When I left I returned the account to Comcast. David's Twitter handle is his name, just like my Twitter handle is now. In that case David should own it, even if some of the followers followed due to David's relationship with Radian 6. There are some gray areas with both of these. Most companies have intellectual rights aspects within their handbook and that is where this would fall. In the court of public opinion, it would be difficult for a company to say that they own someone's name, whereas it is easy to see that the company owns a name that includes the brand. I do expect that more progressive firms will be more open and allow employees who build up a fan base to retain them after leaving even when the handle includes the company name. Of course the company will require the Twitter name to be changed. There is an interesting court case happening now on this exact topic. In the case, Noah Kravitz left his employer, PhoneDog. When he did, he changed his Twitter handle from @PhoneDog_Noah to @NoahKravitz, retaining the approximate 23,000 Twitter followers. There are various accounts of this situation, including some who claim that Noah offered the account to the company, but the company had originally turned it down, only to later follow up with a lawsuit requesting $340,000 in damages, or $2.50 per follower, per month. It will be an interesting case to follow, especially as more details are made public.

Public Relationship Society of America (PRSA) asked Charlene Li, coauthor of *Groundswell* and author of *Open Leadership*, about this on a YouTube video. The video is titled "Charlene Li on Building a Personal Brand While on the Clock." In the video she says that instead of worrying about someone building a personal brand and then leaving your organization, you should celebrate the time that your business has had an opportunity to have that person as part of the team.

One of the big concerns that companies have regarding employees in social media is that at some point the employee may leave, as I did with Comcast. But Comcast's handling of my resignation was absolutely perfect. As an organization, they already had many other employees who were well known in the world of social media. Members of my team were building strong reputations on their own. We announced my departure on the company blog through a post written by me. The organization prepared a heartfelt video including goodbyes from many people whom I had interacted with over the years. The most memorable was seeing Comcast founder Ralph Roberts wishing me well. Comcast then threw a party to celebrate the accomplishments. As I departed, Comcast then focused posts on my team members and their individual accomplishments. The fact is that Comcast is still there for their Customers and the digital care team will continue to be there for their Customers.

Comcast celebrated my time with them as I left and I continue to celebrate my experience with them. The three years that I spent at Comcast were the most amazing and rewarding three years of my career. I built a whole new team to do work never defined before. We worked tirelessly to generate change throughout the organization and make sure the Customer was always our focus. I am so proud of that team, what they accomplished while I was there, and more importantly, what they continue to accomplish. I feel so privileged to have worked with hardworking, dedicated, and passionate people during the adventure and I learned countless lessons from each of them. I treasure this experience and I will remain forever grateful to Comcast and the Comcast Customers.

My decision to leave was based on a number of factors. My background has been in financial services and I had an opportunity to try to drive change within that industry. The main factor that led to the change was the opportunity to do something a little different. The fact is that the snowball is going down the hill at Comcast; change is happening. It may take a long time, but they have the right people and procedures in place to do it. My team was maturing and taking on our tasks with ease.

The changing business environment will require leadership at all companies to build a focus that you are not afraid for the world to see. We are in a much more connected world, so understand that the world will see all of the inner workings of your brand. That will prepare you for what lies ahead. I expect that this will not be hard for CEOs and other senior leaders, but there will be a middle grouping of management that will not be as thrilled with this change. This has to do with the level of control that they have shown over the years, especially internally. They were always cautious about what was shared upward, but, as you know, inevitably it all comes out sooner or later. I also expect that Customer Service will be getting a seat at every table in the years to come, but if that is to happen it may require new leadership or making existing leadership understand the power and ability that they have to steer the organization.

CHAPTER

28

Who Is Your Chief Customer Officer?

It is vital to have someone to help lead the changes happening in our workforce, our brands, and our Customers. The role must be high enough in the food chain to properly advise a CEO on all the topics discussed in this book. Some will say that is the role of the Chief Marketing Officer because they understand the impact these things are having on the brand. To some extent, I agree with that and I expect that many Chief Marketers will step up to the role, and many have already.

However, one of the fastest growing roles in business today is the Chief Customer Officer. This is not a new role, but has been growing over the past fifteen years. We have seen a variety of titles for this position, depending on the organization, such as Chief Client Officer and Chief Customer

Experience Officer, among many others. When we look at the C-Suite, most companies have a Chief Executive Officer, Chief Financial Officer, Chief Marketing Officer, General Counsel, and various product leaders. Their roles are to guide the strategic direction of the organization. All understand the basic functions and advisory capacity that these executives are providing the CEO, and they are each imperative for the success of the business. Who is representing the Customer within this advisory group?

Many will make the case that all the officers should be representing the Customer and the shareholder. That is obviously a nice sentiment but it does not always work out that way. Product people have a passion for their product, which sometimes makes it difficult to see past that or the overall impact that certain decisions may have. In my view, the CFO and the general counsel represent the shareholder by protecting assets or potential legal consequences that decisions may have. The Chief Marketing Officer is often focused on the best manner to position decisions publicly. It is the CEO's role to take all of the information and formulate this into an overall plan for the company.

According to the Chief Customer Officer Council website, the first appointed CCO was Kevin Kahn of the Colorado Rockies in 1998. This made a lot of sense for a relatively young sports team to drive fan growth along with the overall experience of the fan base. From there, we saw the expansion of the CCO role into many other businesses, with most of these changes happening in younger technology firms. The CCO within a technology firm would make sure that the efforts of the engineers were truly generating what Customers wanted. Since then we have watched it hit virtually every industry.

According to the CCO Council, the common goals from this role are:

- Drive profitable Customer behavior: To help Customers spend more, and more often, the CCO must focus on initiatives such as profitability segmentation, Customer retention, Customer loyalty, satisfaction, and improving the Customer experience. As well, many CCOs will use in-depth Customer insight to inform the sales and marketing efforts to acquire more of the right and profitable Customers.

- Create a Customer-centric culture: One of the most important roles of the CCO is to help create a strong, Customer-centric culture complete with accountability and ownership at all levels in the company. CCOs who fail at this imperative incessantly put out fires and burn out as nobody else takes ownership. CCOs must prioritize Customer initiatives to drive the most profitable initiatives with the greatest Customer impact. They must put a face on Customers and help employees (especially the non-Customer-facing employees) remain focused on driving Customer value.

- Delivering and demonstrating value to the CEO, the Board, peers, and employees: Because the CCO role is new and some are not yet fully convinced of the value, the CCO must strive to deliver demonstrable value to all stakeholders, not the least of which are the CEO, the Board, and peers. Because results are sometimes harder or take longer to measure, CCOs must be very clear about their performance metrics to allay concerns about performance. As well, CCOs have to proactively collaborate with some executives who may feel threatened by the CCO's broad purview into Customer issues that span traditional silos.

The CCO council further defines the successful CCO as growing the Customer base, enhancing profitability, increasing the strength of the Customer as an asset, and balancing the C-Suite and Board with their traditional focus on cost cutting and revenue growth.

The CCO often does not have reporting responsibility for every aspect of service, but they do have the voice at the table to guide the strategy of the organization. The challenge as companies grow is that this focus is often lost. In smaller companies, it is easy for a CEO or any other leader to keep up with the Customer experience. They simply walk over to departments that have direct access and chat with them. As companies grow and the silos take hold, it is difficult for these leaders to understand the experience of the Customer, especially when they may cross through various silos. The role of the CCO is to connect those dots. They ensure that the CEO is able to make well-informed decisions for anything that has impact to your Customers. The CCO also sends the right message to your own employees and your Customers. As an organization you care about the Customer! In today's world, there is a distrust of businesses, but part of that has to do with the perception that leaders are out for themselves, not the good of the Customer, society, or even the shareholders. This has been fueled by numerous stories, such as Enron or even the mortgage crisis over the past few years. Businesses can start to rebuild this trust by having someone focus on the Customer's needs.

CHAPTER

29

The Power in You

Before I take the time to bring everything together, I would like to take a few minutes to thank you for taking the time to be a part of this dialogue. I tried to gear this toward all levels within an organization. If you are at the top of your career, I hope that this book provided you with some insight into how your organization has been successful and ways you can lead it in the future. If you are a small business owner, you now know some of the pitfalls that larger organizations have seen and you know how to differentiate your business accordingly. Most of us have achieved our role in business based on our passion, and now is the time to feed it, and let it grow. If you are just starting out in your career, and are getting frustrated with certain things, you should know that you do have the power to change things. No matter the groups that you are part of, you have, and will continue to have, the ability to change the world in a positive way.

If you could not tell, Steve Jobs and Apple have always fascinated me; you may have noticed them mentioned once or twice in different parts of the book. Steve's life was a fascinating and inspirational story that played strongly into the culture of the company. Their products in conjunction with their good Customer experiences have locked me in as a Customer. They are one of the most discussed brands within social media, yet their presence there is very limited, if at all. No matter your view of the company or of the former CEO, Steve's story is worth pondering.

Shortly after Steve left Apple in 1985, he conducted an interview with *Newsweek*. The entire interview is insightful and you begin to understand what would drive Apple upon his return. This quote embodies Steve's view on the Customer:

> I obviously believed in listening to Customers, but Customers can't tell you about the next breakthrough that's going to happen next year that's going to change the whole industry. So you have to listen very carefully. But then you have to go and sort of stow away—you have to go hide away with people that really understand the technology, but also really care about the Customers, and dream up this next breakthrough.

Steve, like all of us, was a product of his history. He grew up in the changing times of the sixties and seventies. This instilled in him the power to question the status quo. At the time when Apple started, he and Steve Wozniak were artists, bringing Apple to life. Steve and Woz envisioned how the computer could, and would, change life for all of us. As time went on, Apple saw a few failures, but Steve learned from his mistakes and soon developed the Macintosh. Then came some tough challenges, which ultimately led to his departure from the company he loved. He chose to pursue other interesting experiences that would continue to help shape him, including the development and eventual sale of NeXT to Apple. He also invested in Pixar, a company that soon after produced some well-loved and well-known movies. Pixar was eventually sold to Disney, making Steve Jobs its largest shareholder.

These experiences guided Steve's artistic passion and vision. He learned what he liked within different corporate cultures and what did not work for him or the companies that he was involved with. He then returned to a damaged Apple. Many thought that Apple would soon be extinct, but Steve and the Apple team proved them wrong. His experiences all came together to create the Apple that we know today.

Steve made tough choices, some of which alienated Apple from others. He was sometimes selective regarding the software that would be on the Apple computers; he even stopped allowing others to create Apple clones. When he did not like the way that companies sold his products, he simply changed the model, which eventually led to the birth of the Apple store. Steve guided product design based on his own likes and dislikes as opposed to basing them on data from focus groups. He had an instinct to what the masses would like. He did not strive to meet everyone's needs, just the needs of everyday people. At times this annoyed people, especially when they felt Apple was controlling what they could do with these tools. The best example was the Apple App Store, which limited what apps would be available for the iPhone and iPod Touch. Overall, Steve was really shaping the user experience, as he placed a large emphasis on ensuring that Customers would have positive experiences with their devices.

Anyway, as I look through Steve's prodigious career, I see a human being who was shaped by experiences. Steve was an intensely passionate person with a mission to "change the world." We may want to put him on a pedestal, but Steve simply embodied what is in many of us. We all have our passions and if we use them in the right manner, we can create some unbelievable things. As an example, my goal is to change the way we think about Customer Service, and I am living that passion by writing this book. But I also do it in every interaction that I am part of, whether that is with a Customer or speaking to leaders. I luckily had the opportunity to work for fascinating leaders over the years who were willing to allow me to live my passion for the Customer.

Each one of us can drive change; the key is finding the manner to do that. If you are looking to drive change in the way your organization cares for Customers, share their stories. Be persistent, yet always respectful. Change will happen. If you are trying to inspire your workforce, embody what you are trying to drive. Live it every day and those around you will follow. Remember that Alex's Lemonade Stand believes that every person can make a difference in the world. Alex Scott made an unbelievable difference for those fighting childhood cancer, and I believe you can make a difference in anything you put your mind to.

CHAPTER

30

The Relationship Hub

Does it sound like Consumers are singing the famous Twisted Sister song, "We're Not Gonna Take It," in stereo? If so, in many ways, you are right! Customers are dissatisfied with unprofessional service, products that don't work, companies trying to sell them products that they don't need, and overall unacceptable service. We have been watching this aggrandize and I expect that it will continue to grow dramatically in the coming years. You can allow this to be a frustration or instead you can see it as an opportunity to thrive.

The way to win in this Consumer-driven environment is to create experiences that would cause your Customers to want to share your story. There is opportunity each and every time that your employees interact with Customers as well as through the products that you produce and the services that you provide. It is really not a new concept. The only difference today is that all Customers have a megaphone with which to share their good and bad experiences. Customers have voices that can reach millions and the scale of the Customer voice now rivals that of other broadcast media, like radio and television. Customers are not looking for you to create a million ways to interact with them or hop onto the latest buzz in Service or Marketing. They would prefer that you create an experience that acknowledges them as a person and values them as a Customer. It is really that easy.

One company that is winning in this Consumer-driven environment is a local supermarket called McCaffrey's, owned by Jim McCaffrey. They are a relatively small company with only three locations; the original location is in Bucks County, Pennsylvania, and two newer stores are in New Jersey. They thrive on providing superior Customer Service; they listen and they go above and beyond to exceed Customer expectations. If you ever need or want something unusual, Jim and his team will order it for you. Not only will they order it, they will actually maintain stock of the item so that you will find it the next time you go in. Over the years the supermarket has become, as the *Buck's County Courier Times* put it, "The Town Center."

In February 2004, the Bucks County store had a fire that interrupted business. For many small businesses this travesty would mean the end, but not for McCaffrey's. The town and the citizens rallied behind McCaffrey's. Townspeople even helped to raise money for employees who would not have the opportunity to work. While the store was being rebuilt, McCaffrey's set up a large tent in their parking lot and reopened their business. The tent store was a success as Customers continued to shop in the tent with the brand that they loved! What makes this more surprising is that there is another popular supermarket chain from the Philadelphia area in a connected parking lot, but the loyalists stayed with Jim and his team. Jim built a truly remarkable relationship hub.

Can you build a McCaffrey's difference with your own Customers? To win in social media, and in Customer Service overall, you simply need to have your employees and Customers rally behind you. They will actively tell their friends to use your business, and it will thrive.

The creation of a relationship hub does not happen overnight, nor does it start with a social media campaign. It first begins with your own employees and your company culture. Respect your employees and respect your Customers in everything that you do.

Those with direct connection to your Customer are at the center of the hub and everything else will flow from there. These hubs can change the way that Customers interact with you and they can change your business. Remember that all communications, whether direct to the Customer or through other channels, such as PR or marketing, will be viewed with Consumer lenses. Your Customer has already been empowered to interpret information, good or bad, and share it with whomever they choose.

Customer Service has failed, but this failure is certainly not due to the people servicing your Customers. It is instead due to the many decisions that have impacted your team. No one wants to provide bad service! The first step to change is honestly evaluating your Customer experience and your employee experience. Do your employees have the tools necessary to accomplish what your Customer demands? What is morale like for your frontline employees? Do your employees have access to the people within the organization that can meet these demands? Do they feel empowered?

How are you communicating with your Customers? Are communications as open as they can be? There will be times when tough business decisions have to be made and implemented. Prices or rates may have to go up, or maybe you are in a risk-based business, and circumstances with a specific Customer have changed. How are you communicating this information? Does the Customer believe in your assessment? Does your Customer believe that everything possible was done before you took negative action? Would other Customers believe it? Does your Customer believe that you are on their side? Communicating in an open and honest way can help with all of this. It may not make everyone happy, but if you build a reputation for being fair, others will defend you.

Unfortunately, many companies do not communicate openly, but it is never too late to try. Now is the time to change that. Your Customers will reward an open and honest dialogue and the respect you are showing them.

As the ideal relationship hub takes shape, you will gain new levels of insight from your Customer Service department and you will see many of the silos start to break down. In businesses with one-on-one interaction, feedback will flow to generate new ideas and new products. You must listen, analyze, and implement change. These new ideas and new products will generate excitement from all those involved in the creation and implementation process, including your front line staff and the Customers they are listening to. This, of course, will lead to increased sales for your business. Employees will enjoy their jobs because they can help drive the direction of the business.

The Customer must sincerely be the center of the relationship. Words are not enough; this must be reality. Your frontline team will recognize this and so will the Customer. Your frontline team will also respect this and treasure their empowerment. Employee morale will soar! When this occurs, your Customers will want to share everything about you and their positive experiences with you in any social circumstance.

All businesses have relationship hubs and this is where they truly define success. These are your frontline employees, your call centers, your salespeople, your volunteers, and anyone else interacting directly with Customers. The hub may also be in your storefront, or website, or elsewhere within social media.

It is where your Customer communications come together. In conjunction with quality products and impeccable service, your relationship hub is where it all meets. Happy employees will create delighted Customers. Satisfied Customers will want to share their experiences with anyone who will listen. Creating a world-class relationship hub is in everyone's best interest and will result in tremendous success for your business.

Index